A Birkenhead Hippie

Walter Hicks

Narrated by his sister

Pauline Hicks

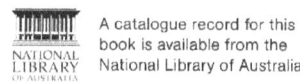
A catalogue record for this book is available from the National Library of Australia

Copyright © 2023 Pauline Hicks
All rights reserved.
ISBN-13: 978-1-922727-78-7

Linellen Press
265 Boomerang Road
Oldbury, Western Australia
www.linellenpress.com.au

Acknowledgment

This book is for the children of the four Hicks kids:
- Carl, Babs' son
- Jill and Peter, Pauline's children
- Matthew and Sarah, Walter's children
- Paula, Katy, and Dawn, Johnson's children.

As parents we wanted you to know your unique history, and then to pass it on to our grandchildren.

With all our love.

When you cease to fear your solitude, a new creativity awakens in you. Your forgotten or neglected wealth begins to reveal itself. You come home to yourself and learn to rest within. Thoughts are our inner senses. Infused with silence and solitude, they bring out the mystery of inner landscape.

Anam Cara – John O'Donohue

Introduction

Walter, my brother, and me.

This book is a collection of writings and historical emails that my brother, Walter, and I (Pauline) shared as we learned our life lessons. We were close and corresponded throughout our lives. Over the latter part of Walter's life, we had begun to draft a story based on some facts of our lives. We wrote of our family life as children up to when we stepped out on our adult journey. From there I had to continue alone by authoring the story of our ruminations in our later years that have resulted in this being half a book and half a monograph. We had an older sister Babs and a younger brother Johnson. We were the two middle kids and as children even looked alike.

    Walter and I relied on each other for emotional and spiritual support and needed to stay connected and so promised we would write to each other regularly even if it were just to say, 'I'm alive.' Being typically Irish, our communications read like stories, and so, fortunately, I printed some of his emails and kept them. Although we were fierce advocates for peace, not war, our personal adult lives were struggling and troubled.

    We were raised right after WW2, amongst the devastation of the bombed infrastructure, and with the people that were mentally and physically damaged. We lived the aftereffects, and Birkenhead's suffering and anger were still rife. Daily we heard stories of how they witnessed death in that war. And so, the war continued for these people which included us kids.

In 1964, Walter donned his Hippie threads at the age of sixteen. He conducted his conscientious, peaceful objections to war for some years in Northern England, Newquay (at least 12 months) London and Spain. He chased love to live in Oregon, America, in the mid-seventies near the end of the Hippie movement. I moved to New Zealand and, eventually, Australia, attempting to start a new life away from an abusive marriage.

We both had two children, a boy and a girl, and they were our priorities in life. They went on to produce five grandchildren for each of us. Our marriages didn't last. Walter and I wrote about how we were managing our 'life' highs and lows and what we learned and shared through our lessons and heartaches. As we moved into our twilight years, we shared our philosophical thoughts about life in general.

In 2021, Walter lost his home, possessions, and writings, including his poetry in the fires of Oregon. Fortunately, I still had some early emails of his work and we had begun to use these as the basis of our book. This is that book, but only two years after losing his life's work, sadly, Walter died on 22nd January 2023. For the following eight weeks, my spiritual brother and I completed this book. I have identified our separate words with our names above each chapter and then continued with our philosophical thoughts about our lives collected from our emails. It wasn't the story we planned when he was here in the flesh, but here now is the 'soul' of the man that was adamant we have Peace, not War.

This is my labour of love to my Hippie brother Walter.

Soul slipping

by Walt Hicks

After the bomb dropped
Only embers remained.
But as you blew them
The embers they flamed.
A flame just erupted.
Like a flash in the night
And my death grip was loosened.
By horror and fright.
My soul slid.
slipped
And tumbled
And then
In silent panic
I don't know when!
I fell into a fresh place
All sparkling with dew.
A new state of being
Had suddenly grew.
New life had erupted
And I'd had no part
In the slipping and sliding
That gave me new heart.
Destroyed by illusion,
Reborn by my dreams,
Now onward and upward
My eternal soul streams.
It's mystery that guides us,
And mystery that gives,
And it's only by mystery
That my immortal soul lives.

World War II in Birkenhead England 1941

The environment into which we were born.

Air raid sirens began to scream and pierce the black starless night sky. Doris, fully dressed for escape, catapulted out of bed, frantic!! Her heart beat out of her chest. She plucked her twelve-month-old baby Sarah from her cot and wrapped her in yet another thick blanket. For the first time in days, Sarah was sleeping comfortably and Doris was thinking:

Why now? You bastard Hitler, why couldn't you give us one clear night so my baby could begin to recover?

Her husband was somewhere out there fighting a war and she wasn't allowed to know where! *He's probably suffering more than me*, she thought. *The world and everyone in it needs strength right now*. Racing out of her house at the bottom of Gamlin Street in Birkenhead, she grabbed the pre-packed shoulder bag, handles thrown over her head, and in terror began to run toward Birkenhead North train station. The door of her friend, Winnie, was open in Buccleuch Street as she bellowed into the hall:

"Winnie, do you need help?" Winnie's husband was also away fighting in the war, and Doris admired how she managed her three children alone. Her middle child had polio and Doris knew she would be locking his leg splints onto him.

"I'm coming, Dot. Go on ... I'll be two minutes." Doris's throat began to restrict her breath as she gripped her baby to her chest and ran panicking, looking into the sky, and vaguely seeing the lights of a fleet of approaching planes in the distance.

Not now, God. Stop them. Not now. Let Winnie and her kids get to safety, she prayed as she ran into the Birkenhead North train tunnel which was now used during the bombing as an air raid shelter. With a quick look back, she could see Winnie and the kids running frantically but were only a minute away. They would make it in time. *Thank you, God.*

The day's rain had created a lake in the tunnel at least twelve inches deep that she paddled through. Small train lamps flickered on the brick arched roof through the middle of the tunnel and away from the entrance, giving enough light to identify faces. The shelter was already packed with people lining the walls as she threaded her way around knees, legs, and feet.

Yuk! Something slimy is wrapping itself around my leg. In alarm, she looked down but calmed quickly seeing it was only a piece of wet newspaper.

A gentle hum of voices filled the air. "Baby coming through. Baby coming through," was a low chant that moved along with Doris as she walked between the crowd of tired faces looking for a place to sit. Some had brought kitchen chairs but carrying Sarah meant that luxury wasn't an option. An elderly gentleman had been sitting on a square brick wall support and he stood saying, "'ere ye are, luv; I can stand."

"Are you sure?" she asked as she peered into his frail face. If she took his seat, would he collapse if the bombs lasted most of the night? She couldn't have that on her conscience. She was about to gracefully refuse as she knew the guilt of her sitting and him standing would haunt her, but just then a younger man stood.

"'Ere luv take this kitchen chair."

"Thanks so much. This is really kind of you both." She smiled nervously. Sarah was awake in her arms and now struggling to breathe again. Doris needed to calm herself and concentrate on

Sarah and how to keep her safe and breathing! The bombs had begun to explode above them as she wrapped the blanket around Sarah's head and ears to smother the sound as best she could. The ground vibrated and shook, the explosions deafening,

BOOM!! ….10, 11, 12 …BOOM! …10, 11, 12 …BOOM! … three close together, while the vicar of St James' Church was praying loudly trying to be heard as he asked God for protection. Fear was suffocating Doris as she silently, but over and over, prayed that they would survive the night. *Please, God, please!* (There are no atheists in air raid shelters.)

It was two weeks since Doris had visited the doctor with her 12-month-old child Sarah who had developed a cough that wasn't clearing. She had been given a small amount of penicillin by the doctor which she had been told was the maximum allowance he could prescribe as the bulk of all medications were going straight out to the troops. Sarah's cough was getting worse and was now rattling on her chest and Doris felt her child had pneumonia. She had planned to take her to the hospital the following day, hoping they could give Sarah something to help her breathe easier.

Sitting in this damp tunnel isn't helping my baby to breathe, she thought even though she had no choice. This thought was stirring guilt for bringing her child into an environment that would harm her even more.

That feckin Churchill! That bloody idiot! In exasperation, her anger tried to replace her guilt as she vented with these thoughts. *Why did he decide to use Cammell Lairds to repair the damaged ships during the war? Birkenhead used to be a sleepy little town but it's all munition factories and supply depots now, a hive of industry day and night. How could he be so crazy as to think the damaged ships wouldn't be identified as ships of war, as they limped into the Mersey from the Irish Sea? How could he get it so wrong?*

Moving toward her out of the darkness she saw Winnie and the kids. Her eldest boy was carrying a chair for his mum, and he set it beside Doris who was automatically rocking her baby in her left arm as her right hand felt Sarah's little chest rattle with each breath she struggled to take.

"How's her breathing, Dot?" Winnie asked with concern in her eyes. Doris almost cried at this direct question because she was terrified her baby would not survive the night.

"I'm frightened, Winnie." She choked back the tears as she looked into Winnie's eyes.

Winnie grabbed Doris's shoulder firmly. "We'll all get through this, Dot. We won't let that bastard Hitler win."

Between the noise of the bombs, conversations circulated. She could hear Mrs Brown's voice.

"Our Mary lives in New Brighton on the top corner of the Mersey and the Wirral, looking out to the Irish Sea, and she was telling me there's a rumour Lord Haw-Haw lives there watching for the ships entering the Mersey and coming here for repairs."

It was discovered soon after the war had finished that Lord Haw-Haw turned out to be William Joyce, a Nazi spy living in Germany. Daily he sent out propaganda messages via radio throughout the war. He once lived with his relatives on the Wirral and it was thought they informed Joyce of the damaged ships sailing into the Mersey, but this couldn't be proved as the source of his information. He was arrested in Germany in May 1945 and accused of high treason. He was hanged on January 3rd, 1946. William Joyce was born Irish.

"That toe rag has told Hitler all about this area," another joined in the conversation.

"Whoever he is has built a radio station in his attic and he's lettin' the Germans know about the damaged ships comin' into Cammell Lairds."

"Did you hear him on the radio this afternoon tellin' us all in his nasal voice - Germany calling, Germany calling, Hitler will make the blood run down the seven roads of St James Church tonight and raze the buildings to the ground. Haw Haw Haw." I wanted to pick up the radio and smash it to pieces on the kitchen floor!"

"He's thinkin' he's bein' humane," said another, "warning us so we can get into the air raid shelters early. But people are still being killed because of him, the bastard!"

"Yes, Hitler is trying to destroy those ships, but he even knows about the munition factories and supply depots that have been built here. That's why he's determined to wipe us off the face of the earth. Everything is neatly packaged in one place for him and marked by the Church. It's like Churchill wrapped us up in a bundle and handed us over to Hitler."

St James' Church sat on a central roundabout near the docks and had seven roads splaying out from it. From the air, this was a clear landmark for the planes as it would look like a wheel sitting on the docks. All the munition factories and supply depots had been built on any spare land on these roads. It was therefore important for Germany to wipe this part of England off the map. Unfortunately, all the locals also lived here.

Winnie and Doris began chatting, trying to hide the fear they both felt. They wanted the children to see and hear normal conversation to help them not feel too frightened through the night. Sarah's face was becoming ashen and losing its colour. Doris willed each breath as she looked into her child's face.

"Not long now, Dot, and you can take her straight to the hospital when we get out. I'll get me Dad to take ye in the lorry."

"Thanks, Winnie. That would really help (then whispering so the children didn't hear) I hope everyone managed to get into the tunnel tonight 'cos I don't think I can take another morning identifying those that died. I honestly do dread that scene as much as being here listening to the bombs."

Emerging from the air raid shelters was one of the nightmares everyone dreaded – not only because they weren't sure if their home was still standing, but because the bodies of the dead were lined up along the streets with sacks covering their faces and a slate and chalk at their head. This had been carried out by the Air Raid

Wardens. Once they had laid the dead in the streets in this way, they then sounded the all-clear siren. Everyone's duty out of respect for those who died was to identify the dead. They had to lift the sack away from their face and if they recognized the person, they would print the name on the slate. They also had to read the names of everyone on the slates to discover who didn't make it through the night. Dread engulfed Doris each time and her body movements always felt automated and surreal as she lifted the sacks praying that it wasn't anyone she knew. This also became a recurring nightmare for most inhabitants. This was torture!

Rocking! Rocking! "Shh! Shh! Go to sleep, my baby," she quietly sang looking into her baby's face, but Sarah's little chest still rattled in her struggle to breathe. Doris's hand lay on her baby's chest checking for each breath as she rocked and prayed and willed her to survive. And then … "Oh, my God! My God!" she uttered when she didn't feel her little chest rising to breathe. She stood up with Sarah in her arms.

"A doctor!! A doctor!" she began screaming. Immediately all in the tunnel fell silent and looked in her direction. "A doctor! A doctor!" she screamed even louder. From some distance down the tunnel, a man began running toward her, vaulting over and around people as he shouted.

"I'm a doctor, luv, I'm coming."

People moved out of his way as best they could, allowing him a clearer path. She was now howling into the face of this man as he leaned in to hear Sarah's breathing, but there was no breathing. His eyes swiftly met Doris' and she understood what they were saying. She immediately went into a quiet shock. He first checked visually, then placed his ear on Sarah's chest, and to be sure, he then used his stethoscope as she stood holding her baby. Winnie was repeating a mantra as she gripped Doris' shoulders.

"Please, God, no, please God no, please God no," but too late. The doctor looked mournfully into Doris' eyes and shook his head.

Sarah had died in her mother's arms.

The all-clear was sounding as Doris left the tunnel, still clutching her deceased child and walking like a zombie. She had a rock sitting in her chest and ice in her gut. Her throat was bursting as it held back the tears that she could not or would not release. People milled around her, all saying how sorry they were, but Doris didn't respond. They were merely voices, all talking over one another, a cacophony not making any sense. The doctor steered her toward his car while saying he would take her to the hospital. Doris merely allowed him to move her. Once in the hospital, it took almost an hour for them to complete the official paperwork, and as they covered Sarah's beautiful little face and peeled her out from her mother's arms, only then did Doris release a tsunami of grief that had sat in her gut, dammed back by her throat. As it spewed forth, it violently shook her body with every breath she took.

Her husband was informed and given compassionate leave of three days to attend Sarah's funeral. Doris's emotional support from then on was her friends and family. Nightly, fear-filled, she ran to the air raid shelters; mornings were the torturous ritual of identifying the dead. Doris learned how to be selfless throughout this war. She healed somehow by being strong, genuinely caring about those suffering around her, and keeping busy helping all her neighbours as best she could.

As she relived these stories to her children, she spoke about those worse off than herself. One night as she ran to the tunnel she arrived and looked back to see her friend Winnie and her three children only just leaving their home and beginning to run frantically – Doris looked up to the sky when she heard the whistling of a bomb falling. Horrified she began shouting.

"Faster, Winnie, faster," but she wasn't fast enough. Winnie and her kids perished, right in front of her eyes.

During that war, Doris suffered bombings, witnessed death,

and had to identify body parts – but worst of all she had lost her only child at that time. She continued to live with the memories and endure the aftermath of the atrocities she had witnessed as she raised four more children, also supporting her husband and her neighbours in the community to simply survive another day, another week.

Her husband and many of these men returned from the war suffering shell shock, which is now called post-traumatic stress disorder, (PTSD) but wasn't recognized as such at that time, and counselling wasn't even heard of then. Neighbours supported each other. The women in this community were strong, uncomplicated, selfless, and hardworking. Doris became the rock they offloaded to; her common sense, empathy, and compassion helped them draw the strength to face another day.

Birkenhead was bombed relentlessly throughout the war with the death of over 4,000 residents and more than 2,000 seriously maimed and many buildings and homes destroyed.

Divorce was never considered an option and was never even discussed by the women living after the war in this vicinity. If by chance it did enter their heads after periods of physical violence at the hands of their men (who were deemed mentally disturbed after the war) it would have been dismissed immediately - they would think of divorce as cowardly and weak. They never surrendered, never walked away, and never gave up.

Young females born after the war and raised by these women in our village, learned quickly that stoicism is necessary and women's lives should be sacrificial.

What these women in Birkenhead endured never even reached a page in a history book, but Doris and those women that banded together to form our community, were the true heroes of the second world war.

Doris was our mother. She was born the seventh daughter of the seventh daughter. This, in pagan terms, meant she had prophetic vision; she was a psychic and a clairvoyant. She was only nineteen years old when she lost her first child. That pain plus the experience of surviving the war was her baptism of fire. She became wise at an early age.

She had an aura and empathetic essence that drew people to her for emotional support. She also opened the minds of her children and taught them all she knew about the spirit world.

Our mother and our female neighbours formed the 'community' we were raised in. The men were returned soldiers and were to be cosseted. We kids played amongst the bombed buildings and often unexploded bombs were found amongst the rubble. We grew up hearing the verbal history of war and death which formed the backdrop of our education for life, and the reason this generation of kids, born from the war years onward, cried "Peace, not War."

St James' Church in Birkenhead North

Being born and first memories

Walter

We don't just materialize into life after a puff of smoke and the word Abracadabra, nor do we easily come to the realization that we are alive. If we did we could ask, what happened? Then maybe someone would answer, "You've been born! You're alive!" But then if we inquired further and asked, "Why?" … the most we would get out of anyone by way of an answer would be a blank look, a shrug of the shoulders, and the words, "Don't ask me, I just live here."

The force behind the miraculous creation of life seems to go about its work at a snail's pace. Life creeps up on us so slowly that at first, we don't even realize that we are *alive*, in fact, the realization that we are *alive* sometimes takes half a lifetime, or even a whole lifetime to achieve. Not me though.

I'm told that it was a sunny June day in the year 1948 when the unknown force pushed me out of a small but very serene bubbling and gurgling world and into a world with much scarier sounds and equally scary sensations. It was in a pub, and to a chorus of loud drunken cheers that I made my entrance, and only seconds after an unexploded bomb was detonated by the army. My mother was in the pub for safety because our house was in danger of being damaged by the blast. The bomb went off, and my mum always said that I was born because of the shock of it!

The other children in our neighbourhood were told that they were found under a gooseberry bush, but not me, my parents were from Ireland. The Irish have a thing about making a story sound a bit better, and as a result, I spent many innocent years thinking that a loud bang meant that another baby had just popped into life.

Whatever the truth of the matter or however it came about, life, for some inexplicable reason, was suddenly mine. The miraculous event must have been very traumatic for me because all memory about being born had been completely obliterated from my conscious mind. It wasn't until I was about four or five years old that the realization slowly dawned on me that I was *alive,* and living in a small murky town called Birkenhead which was situated in the northern part of a country called England. I don't know where I'd lived before being *alive* but felt sure I'd know by the time I was grown up like Mum and Dad.

My childhood was a time when children were still free to wander around the streets to their heart's content, and it was with immense pleasure, with no qualms at all, that I took advantage of the situation very soon after I learned to walk. However, Borough Road, a busy main highway that ran through our community, soon became the bane of my life.

A grand marble building stood on the other side of Borough Road and people called it the General Library. It had walkways all around it with benches scattered here and there, and it just stood there! like a mountain does, doing nothing but looking fantastic, and somehow attracting to it all those that are attracted to such inanimate wonders.

The General Library was the first of many dangerous attractions that came close to robbing me of this miracle of life. The danger came from Borough Road. The cars weren't too bad; they could weave around me or come to a screaming stop. But it was the buses that had me worried. Most of the bus drivers must have learned how to drive in the army because they drove fast, with a sense of urgency, like they were avoiding the mines or something. Sometimes they would only slow down to a crawl on approaching a bus stop and the young and nimble would always jump off, but the older folk often had to scream like bloody murder before the bus driver would finally come to a halt. The drivers had the attitude they were doing you a favour by coming to a full stop. Sitting on the bus was an education of the profanities of the English language at almost every bus stop.

We lived in one of the prefabricated houses the government had built in and around Birkenhead for the returning warriors of the war. The original houses in Carnforth Street had been bombed and the prefabs were built when most of the demolition of the remains was cleared. Our next-door neighbour was Mister Fairhead who was known far and wide as old Pearhead. He was the first person that showed me just how fragile life is.

Every day at five minutes to one o'clock all the neighbourhood children would gather outside old Pearhead's prefab. At one o'clock, a loud air raid siren would wail to announce to the men working in Cammell Lairds that it was time to return to work after their lunch hour. It reminded many people of the war and especially those that had returned with their nerves shattered after their experience. Old Pearhead hadn't realized the war was over and would come running out of the door of his prefab holding his buttocks and screaming in fright. If one of our parents were around, they would grab him and take him back to his house, soothing him and settling him down again. If he wasn't stopped, then with long loping strides he would run down the hill to Borough Road, where the speeding cars and buses would make him change direction and almost always he would turn left.

My parents made me call him Mister Fairhead. They said he was ill and 'bomb happy.' They told us that many people couldn't stand the sound of the bombs exploding and that they'd taken leave of their senses, and with this explanation, we were told they deserved our respect. I didn't know what they were talking about but I felt enormously proud about having such a well-known bomb-happy celebrity living right next door to me and often boasted of it.

Then I overheard a conversation between Mum and Dad talking about the town council stopping the use of the air raid sirens because people were being reminded constantly of the war years. They had replaced it with the firing of a loud cannon. I liked the idea of a child being born every time the men had to go back to work, *but how will this affect old Pearhead?* I thought.

The next day at one o'clock I decided not to join the usual crowd of giggling children outside old Pearhead's prefab. I looked out the window at the children and felt sorry for them as I felt they wouldn't see old Pearhead running again, I was sure they were going to be disappointed. Suddenly the cannon boomed and our windows rattled, the children were scattering and screaming with delight as old Pearhead came loping out of his house holding his buttocks and wearing only tattered underpants. He followed his usual path downhill to Borough Road but this time he didn't turn left. He stopped, and with wide horrified eyes, he looked back at his wife and prefab. Then still holding his buttocks he turned and ran straight into the path of a number 76 bus.

It was the first real shock of my very young life. I watched with wide-eyed fascination as the traffic came to a halt. A crowd gathered and a man took off his coat and put it over old Pearhead's body. His wife was screaming and hysterical as other women tried to comfort her. A police car arrived and was soon followed by an ambulance and old Pearhead's body was placed carefully on a stretcher and then taken into the ambulance. After a short while the traffic began moving again and within minutes Borough Road was just as busy as usual as if it hadn't happened.

Explosions had always meant the beginning of life to me but now I felt confused. This most recent loud bang resulted in a death. It got me thinking! Why was it that after all that time of being afraid of air raid sirens, old Pearhead met his death because of a cannon and a bus? I concluded that he had wasted a lot of time worrying over the wrong thing.

Nobody I had known had ever died before and I needed to know why? If the government people didn't want to upset folk, then why did they use the cannon and not the siren and make old Pearhead die?

I was shocked.

My first attempt at 'really' thinking only resulted in more confusion, and as I tossed and turned that night in bed beside my sisters, I came to another drastic and scary conclusion. *Could it be?* I thought, *could it be that everyone is a wee bit bomb happy?*

The Birkenhead Library on Borough Road.

Childhood

Pauline

The light of dawn began to creep around the edge of the curtains and into my bedroom and, as I opened my eyes, I immediately thought, *It's t'morreh! Mum said we were going on holiday t'morreh and that is now.* The excitement fluttered my tummy and I had to go to the toilet.

"Yer like a wee puppy," my father would often say, and it was true. Every time I got excited, I nearly wet myself. I came out of the bathroom now bursting with my excitement and fighting to control it. I very slowly and quietly opened my parent's bedroom door. With my hand still on the doorknob, I peered at the back of Mum's head as it lay on her pillow, saying nothing and willing her to wake up. Mum slowly turned to look at me as I stood there in my nightie.

"It's t'morreh now, isn't it, Mum? Can I get ready t'go on holidays?" I half whispered, not wanting to be loud as Mum would tell me so many times the rules of mornings are to be quiet and slow! I was still trying hard to learn these rules.

"Oh, luv, it's not even six o'clock yet; we're not going 'till six o'clock t'night; go back t'bed," she moaned.

I slowly closed the door, thinking, *how can she go back t'sleep when she knows she's goin' on holiday?*

I began skipping with my excitement, as I wasn't allowed to run, and I skipped back into my bedroom. "I'll put my best frock on now then I'll be ready before anyone else," and a squeal was playing in my chest that I wasn't allowed to let out. As I was always first to wake up Mum had told me last night to quietly pack my bag as I waited for the others.

The small bag Mum had given me to pack my clothes in lay on the floor. I carefully went through all the clothes I owned and placed anything without a hole in it in the bag.

Most of my clothes were hand-me-downs from my sister, but that didn't matter to me. When she got new clothes, I would get as excited as she did, because I knew I would get them eventually. My doll – that used to belong to my sister but I wasn't supposed to know; and had appeared in my Christmas stocking with a new frock on and her face washed – sat looking at me from my bed. I loved my doll and I wasn't sure if she was allowed to come with me. "It might be expensive to take dolls on holiday, Sally, but I'll ask if you can go?" I whispered to her. Back I went to the door of my parent's bedroom and slowly opened it again. Mum looked over at me.

I screwed my face and eyes and crunched my head down into my shoulders showing I wasn't sure if I might be able to do this as I asked, "Can Sally come on holiday with us, Mum? Or is it too expensive for her?" My words were sheepish as I prepared myself for a no.

"Yes, luv, take 'er if ye want to, now don't come back again until I get up." She sighed.

Oh! My squeal nearly popped out of my mouth! I closed the door and excitedly hopped and skipped back into my bedroom and picked Sally up and hugged her as I danced around the room. "You can come with us on holiday, Sally. You can meet my Nana and Grampa, and play with the wee pigs, and run in the fields, and we'll see the hens, and the beautiful swans on the lake, an EVERYTHIN'!! AND!!! We are goin' on the big boat t'get there. Ooooh! It's goin' t'be lots of fun," I whispered as I wrapped her in my arms trying hard not to wake my brother and sister.

Once my bag was packed it seemed like such a long time since I had woken up that I felt if my brother and sister didn't wake up soon they might be too late for our holiday. I peered right into the face of my little brother, Walter, and pressed my nose against his as he started to wake. "Come on, wee sleepy head," I whispered excitedly. "It's t'morreh!"

Our grandparents owned a pig farm in Moneyreagh, County Down in Northern Ireland. Cammell Lairds, where Dad worked building ships, closed for two weeks every year on the last week in July and the first week in August. This was when we took our holidays. Mum would save all year round, and with Dad's holiday pay, we could usually afford to get the Irish Ferry across to Belfast and spend two weeks with our grandparents.

My world was measured in two halves. The two most precious moments in my life were Christmas and Holidays. As soon as one was over, I counted the days until the other arrived.

We must be the luckiest people on earth to 'ave a Nana and Grampa in Ireland, I thought; and pitied the rest of humanity.

"Don't ye go boastin' now, wee girl; that poor wee lass can 'ardly afferd a lace fer 'er shoe," my dad would say if he caught me bragging. So I was supposed to keep it to myself and say nothing, and I didn't know how anybody else did it! It was the hardest thing in the world for me to contain my excitement about anything I felt passionate about, and I felt passionate about a lot of things.

Sitting on the steps of our house with my bag packed, my best frock on, and Sally sitting beside me, I waited … just waited … for somebody to come along that I could boast to. I knew I would have to say it quietly in case my dad heard me, and the first person I could tell came around the corner.

Jumping off the steps, I ran to meet her and excitedly whispered in her ear, "We're goin' overseas on holiday to Ireland!" She stepped back and smiled while she looked at me.

"Now?" she said.

"No, t'night at six o'clock, *and* we're goin' on the ferry boat … the big one that goes t' Ireland!" I squealed in excitement and jumped up and down. I wanted to go to the toilet again but not until I had finished boasting; so I put my hands between my legs and crossed them; then bounced on the spot.

"Yer lucky thing ye!" said my friend, "a wish I 'ad a Nan in Ireland" Then she looked sad, and I knew what my dad meant, and I felt sorry for her.

"Not everybody has a Nan in Ireland; we're just very, very, very lucky, that's all. I'll tell yer all about it when a get back, an' it'll be just like ye' went." I had lost a bit of my spark now and I felt guilty for making my friend sad. "I'll 'ave t'go now 'cos a want a wee. I'll see ye when a get back." And I ran indoors to the toilet before I wet myself.

It's really hard being happy and not sharing it with someone in case you make them sad, I thought as I sat on the toilet; but I soon bounced back and sat on the steps again, waiting for my next 'victim'.

The Irish Ferry boat set sail for Belfast at midnight, but the six o'clock departure time my mother had given us for leaving the house seemed like it would never arrive.

"Come on," my mother shouted from inside the house. "It's time to go." I jumped off the step squealing with pleasure and gave a little dance on the spot.

We began to walk down the street to Borough Road where we would get the bus to the Birkenhead Ferry. We would then take the ferryboat across the Mersey to Liverpool where the Irish Ferry boat was docked.

My father was at the head of the procession, his small frame tipped to one side as he carried a large heavy suitcase that he tried hard not to drag on the ground. My mother followed carrying my little brother Walter in one arm and a bag over the other; my sister Babs walked behind my mother and I brought up the end of the procession. Wanting to be like Mum, I carried my precious Sally in one arm and my bag of clothes in the other, but I had to skip along behind because I found it impossible to walk.

The entire neighbourhood seemed to spill out of their doors with everybody shouting goodbye to us. "Have a good 'oliday. See ye when yiz get back; we will look after the 'ouse, don't worry. Hope the weather keeps fine fer yiz all."

And I waved to everybody and quietly squealed with pleasure.

At the bottom of our street on Borough Road, we boarded the double-decker bus and Dad placed the heavy suitcase under the stairs; the bus conductor rubbed the top of my head and said, "Goin' on 'oliday, are ye, little un?"

"Yes!" I beamed "To Ireland t'see me Nanna and Grampa."

The seats on the bus were placed two abreast and my mother and father sat behind me and my sister, with Walter on Mum's knee. Babs had brought her book and began reading, but sitting still in the seat was impossible for me. I fidgeted my bum, stood up, and looked around, kneeling on the seat. I leaned over toward Mum and Dad, gently pinching my little brother's cheek.

"We're on our way, we'll soon be there," I sang.

"Will you sit down, Pauline. Yer makin' me dizzy," my mother ordered. Oh, I found it really hard to sit still when I was excited; I didn't know how to do it.

As I sighed and slumped down into the seat, I raised my legs in front of me. They reached the back of the next seat. I pushed my feet against it and the back of my seat snapped back. If I pushed my feet and straightened my legs, I could fit tightly into this space between the seats. Each time I did it the back of my chair went back and then immediately snapped forward, throwing me toward the back of the seat in front of me. So I did it again, and again, and again … until my mother said, "Get your feet off that chair and sit still, will you!"

Oh, this really was the hardest part of goin' on holiday.

Eventually, we reached the ferry and we could see the water.

The bus turned into the terminal and Mum told my sister and me to get off and stand on the kerb until Dad had got the case off the bus.

We walked into the Birkenhead Ferry terminal where Dad bought the tickets, then we stepped onto the floating ramp and Babs and I skipped in excitement down to the water's edge.

The Ferry Boat, which was called *Woodchurch*, was a magical sight to me.

"Get hold of my frock you two 'till we're on the boat," Mum said. And I stood looking up at this beautiful old wooden ferry boat and thought to myself, *My Dad's probably built this!*

Dad led the way onto the gangplank; Mum followed with Walter in her arms, and my sister Babs and I brought up the rear holding onto the hem of her skirt. As I bounced on the balls of my feet holding Mum's frock at the end of the procession, I felt like a bridesmaid at a wedding.

"Now don't go near the rails without ye father," Mum said. "An' stay where I can see ye."

The ropes were thrown back onto the boat. The engines increased in power and the ferry boat left the dockside and chugged its way across the Mersey to Liverpool.

"Should we go an' see the sailors doin' their washin'?" said Dad to Babs and me.

"Yes!!" we screamed, and danced beside him holding his hand as we moved toward the rear of the boat. I grabbed the rail tight and looked over at the foam and spray that came from the back of the boat as it cut its way through the water. Dad had told us that in the bowels of the boat, the sailors scrubbed their clothes, and the foam was the dirty soapy washing water that was draining away.

They must have an awful lot of washin', I thought.

Liverpool loomed in front of us. The large grey sandstone buildings with the eagle on top always made me feel as though I was entering a foreign land.

The Irish Ferry boat, *The Ulster Monarch*, sat further down the dock and was even more impressive than the boat we had just got off. It ascended from the water, a monster dwarfing all around it, and the people looked like ants swarming all over it. The gangplank was wider than the last one, but longer and climbed much higher, and again we had to hold Mum's frock as we walked up to the top of this huge boat. Everybody knew my dad, and shouts of "Hello there, Wally!" seemed to be coming from all around us as I walked, this time like a princess up the gangplank to the deck. I felt so important it was bursting out of me.

Everybody was Irish, and their beautiful singsong voices filled the air, shouting instructions and directions around the boat. We were taken to a cabin that had two sets of bunk beds on either side of the small room. My father placed the case and bags under the bottom bunks.

"I want to sleep on that bottom bunk," Babs said.

"Ay, ye can do that and Walter can be at the bottom end," Dad said.

"And which bed will ye be wantin' t'sleep in t'night?" Dad asked me with a huge grin on his face.

"That top one," I said with excitement.

"Well now, put Sally t'bed in case ye lose 'er," said Mum, and I climbed the narrow little ladder to the top bunk and placed Sally between the sheets, and pulled the covers around her chin.

"You stay there, Sally, cos I've got t'go with the grownups t'night t'have a beer," I told her importantly. We then all went up to the deck to inspect the ship.

"You two hold hands on the ship and don't go wandering off without being able t'see me and ye Dad," Mum told me and Babs

The atmosphere was magical. Everybody was happy and laughing. All these people were going on holiday just like us, so I couldn't make anyone unhappy by letting my enthusiasm out. Babs and I walked behind my mother, each holding onto our side of her skirt and holding each other's hand, looking up at the lovely Irish smiles that were all around us.

After inspecting the ship, we went to the bar where Dad was surrounded by all his friends. The dark of the night drew in and all the different coloured lights went on and the music began.

This created a different atmosphere. Laughter and cigarette smoke, the smell of tar and the sea, singing and dancing, piano accordions, whistles, and drums playing; and the night air swirled about my head and made me giddy with euphoria. Midnight arrived and we had been allowed to stay up to watch the boat leave the dock. I was surprised at how quiet the engines were as they steadily began to thump-thump-thump and move this monstrous vessel with all these happy people on board out to cross the Irish Sea.

As we stood waving from the ship to those standing on the dock a great roar of delight swept around the ship throughout the passengers, and we all then went back inside to the bar where the music began again. Everybody was singing. We knew all the songs because Dad had taught us them. So we sang along as we sailed through the dark on this magical illuminated Christmas tree, all on our way to a fairyland.

This was holiday.

Forcing myself to stay awake as long as I could was hard, and I was woken by my dad, who picked me up from the floor where I sat against the wall.

"Come on, me beauty, it's bedtime fer you."

Dad carried me down to our cabin, while I dozed on his shoulder, and lifted me into my bunk bed beside Sally. Walter and Babs were already fast asleep on the bottom bunk and Dad kissed me goodnight. The light was switched off and he left. The small porthole at the side of my bunk had moonlight streaming through it; it lit the cabin with its pale-yellow eerie glow. The water was swish…swish…swishing against the side of the boat as it rocked from side to side. The engines thump-thump-thumped to a heartbeat rhythm. The muffled singing and laughter and music all wrapped their magic around me and transported me to another dimension.

I am the luckiest wee girl in the whole wide world, NUTHIN' could ever be better than this, ever… ever… ever… I thought as I drifted off into my fairy-tale dreams.

"Oh! I nearly forgot. Thanks very much, God, it's luvly. Eh! Men?"

Pauline as a child, aged 4.

Childhood Christmas

Pauline

On my immediate return from my Ferry Boat and Ireland holiday, I would begin counting down to Christmas.

I was always awake on Christmas morning while it was still dark but, lying perfectly still, hoping Father Christmas had already been, yet knowing if I was awake and he found out he wouldn't stop at our house, so I squeezed my eyes tight shut so he wouldn't know. I was aware of my heart beating as my excitement built. As soon as the light of day began to brighten our bedroom, I catapulted myself out of bed!

Yesterday was one of nearly the absolute best days of my life as we prepared for Father Christmas to visit our house and leave presents. Father Christmas is so very busy on Christmas Eve as he zooms around the world on his sleigh with his magic reindeer that can fly. Dad says he gets a bit tired now and again so he sometimes stops at a very special house and has a beer and a mince pie.

"Oh, I hope he's picked our house!" I squealed.

Last night we had taken three of Dad's biggest woollen working socks, ones without holes in them, and hung them on the mantle shelf over the fireplace for Father Christmas to fill them for us – one for my big sister Babs, one for my little brother Walter and one for me. I had insisted that my name was pinned to my sock because I knew that my little brother had been naughty last week, and if he was going to get ashes in his stocking, I wanted to be sure there was no mix-up between the socks. Mum kept saying that

Father Christmas always knows which sock belongs to which child because he's magic, but I knew my little brother had been _very_ naughty, so I almost cried while insisting that my name went on my sock.

Dad turned me by my shoulders and said sternly, "Now then, wee lass, yer'll be showin' ye Irish paddy here, an' I don't think Father Christmas will be impressed," as he lowered his chin and lifted his eyebrows in disapproval, but he still did it for me: my name was printed on the back of an envelope that had been delivered with a Christmas card in it, and pinned to the toe of one of the socks.

Mum put one of her homemade mince pies on one of our very best china plates and put it on the tray she uses when special people are visiting. Dad placed a bottle of beer beside the pie and the tray was placed on the hearth for Father Christmas to see when he came down the chimney. He doesn't get burnt because Mrs Christmas makes him a special fireproof suit to wear each year that she sews with magic cotton to do the job.

There was a different quiet this morning. The light in our bedroom was different as well. Instinctively I ran to the window, parted the curtains, and the sight caught my breath in my throat as I became bewitched by the scene before me. The world was covered in a pure white blanket of snow. The whiteness lay on the ground, hung in the trees, and covered the rooftops. The transformation was magical. The earth was covered in a white fur blanket.

A squeal of pleasure started in my stomach, and as it began its journey up through my body to my throat, it engulfed my whole being with a feeling of total joy and burst out through my mouth as I squeezed my eyes, smiled my face, and hugged this feeling all around me. I ran to the living room and gasped again in awe! The first thing I noticed was the tray with an empty bottle of beer and a plate. Leaning against the bottle was an envelope with writing on it that looked a bit like my dad's writing and later Dad read it for us. It said, "Thank you, from Father Christmas."

The socks were filled and were now laying on the hearth, each lying on top of a present. One each for all three of us.

Oh!! He's been and he picked our house to rest in' OH!! I squealed aloud as I clapped my hands and did a little dance on the spot. I desperately needed a wee before I opened my presents and ran to the bathroom trying to make me wee quickly. Then ran into our bedroom to wake Walter and Babs. I peered into my brother's little face as I loudly whispered, "Father Christmas has been, Walter. Come and see what he's brought you." Placing my arms around Walter s little chubby body, I carried him into the living room. My brother was one and a half years old now and great fun to share things with. He was still sleepy as I sat him on the floor in front of his present and sock. "Look!" I said excitedly "It's from Father Christmas for you" His eyes lit up and a big smile began to cover his sleepy face as he sat looking at a wooden train and then at me. "Go on, look in your sock … it's yours,' I squealed and smiled, enjoying his reaction.

I fell to my knees beside him and moved my sock with my name on it from the top of a big brown teddy bear, he had one shiny brown eye and one brown button eye, and a paper blue and gold dicky bow around his neck.

"Oh! You are beautiful!" I exclaimed as I picked up this magical present and hugged him to my body. I looked over at Babs' sock sitting on top of two books. "Babs, he's been!" I shouted and began to empty my sock on the floor.

"Empty your sock, Walter, as I did," and we discovered we both had an apple, an orange, a tube of Smarties, and a bag of jellybeans. I did feel relief when I didn't have any ashes in my sock after losing my paddy last night. I looked at my brother's sock and he didn't have ashes either so I guessed that Father Christmas must have been too busy to have noticed us both being naughty. *Whew! That was a relief.*

Mum and Dad and my big sister Babs appeared in the doorway. They were all smiling, and Dad put his arms around Mum and gave her a big smackaroo kiss. I loved seeing Mum and Dad do that. It always made me smile and feel happy inside. Then they all sat on the floor with us and gave us all smackaroo kisses as well. Babs opened her books and, smiling, she looked at me, saying, "I'll read you a bedtime story from this book tonight." I was so happy I merely sat for a while in the middle of all this love and grinned and squealed with some happy tears coming out of my eyes.

"G'way wid ye," said Dad with a big smile as he tweaked my cheek and wiped a tear from it. "Tell me ye teddy bear's name t'be?"

"I don't know yet," I replied. "I want a wee first," and I jumped up, grabbed my new teddy bear, and ran to the bathroom. I placed him on the floor and sat looking at him as I sat on the toilet. *Freddie*, I thought. *His name is Freddie.*

After our breakfast, Mum cleared the kitchen and began cooking the Christmas dinner. Hearing a knock at the front door, I hurriedly ran to open it to our first visitors of the day. My Auntie Winnie was there in her real fur coat – she was my mum's sister and she always gave us presents. My dad said she lived in the posh part of town but didn't wear any knickers.

"Here's your Winnie," he would say to Mum when he saw her walking toward our house from the road. "Fur coat and no drawers." Mum told me it would be rude to repeat that to her, so I never told her I knew she didn't have any knickers.

By the end of the afternoon, all my aunts, uncles, and cousins were congregated in our house. After our Christmas dinner, we gathered around the piano where Dad played and led us into singing all the Christmas carols. In between renditions of carols, he would sometimes do silly noises on the piano, playing out-of-tune songs and singing alone until he found the right note. "Oi've never had one lesson," he would shout as he played this out-of-tune racket. "Oi discovered I had dis wonderful talent and taught meself to play by ear, though I did 'ave to learn to do it wid me fingers as me 'ead started to hurt when I played with me ears! Oi dedicates this next song to me luvly wife," he'd announce. Then he'd start to play an out-of-tune racket and sing, "She was! She was!" Over and over, nothing else! They were the only words. But somehow the tone of his voice and his body movements meant something different with every version of, 'She was.' Everybody was falling about laughing and Mum was using the corner of her apron to wipe away her happy tears.

At 7 o'clock that night as I sat in the corner listening to all this happiness, I was tired, and my head kept falling onto Freddie because it was trying to go to sleep without the rest of me. Mum picked me up and hugged me to her cushions and whispered in my ear, "My wee girl's had a big day; come on sleepy head it's time for bed."

She carried me to bed and put Sally on one side of me and Freddie on the other and kissed me good night. I loved the smell of Mum: it was face powder and lifebuoy soap, and I thought she was the prettiest person I'd ever seen. I was so lucky to have her as my mum.

From my comfy bed, I could still faintly hear the singing and laughter, and though I wished I could stay awake and be with them all, I knew my mum was right. I was too tired even to say my prayers aloud, but I remembered to say thank you in my head before I went to sleep. Mum and Dad had told us that God and Father Christmas could hear a silent thank you in your head so I always did that before I went to sleep. And I added, this *was the best Christmas ever so thank you for that too.*

Babs aged 7 & 47. Her name was Doris and her married name was Robinson. Sadly, Babs died 2nd April 2003

Carnforth Street Lifestyle
1950-1954

Pauline

It was sure to be a Saturday night; the time would be around midnight, and I was four or five years old. I was woken from my sleep and lifted out of bed.

"Come on, me beauty. I want ye t'watch ye father beat the shit outa 'this feller.'"

With my Irish red hair all tousled, and the sleep still gritty in my green eyes, I was carried into the living room wearing only my night dress.

The neighbours and most of the drinkers from the local pub, *The Happy Valley*, which was on the bottom corner of our street, were gathered around the perimeter of our living room where they had been called to witness my father 'beat the shit' out of this man. Dad had been insulted by something this man had said in the pub and so had 'offered him outside' to sort it out. The police had moved them on and so Dad had brought him home to fight him there.

Dad normally stood five feet two inches in his stocking feet, but tonight he believed he had grown another foot in stature, as he did most Saturday nights after *a belly full of ale*, as Mum would often state when he'd been drinking.

A wingback chair was pulled to the front of the audience and I was placed on this to give me a ringside seat. Dad assumed his boxing pose, legs bent at the knees and straddled wide, back straight, and arms held with fists lined up in front of his nose. He had removed his shirt and his 'Persil white vest' had a hole beneath one arm. Mum was tutting to the other females in the audience about him letting her down, "taking off his shirt when he's got an old vest on!" It was one of two that he owned.

His thick leather belt with a large brass buckle was tight around his waist holding up his trousers, and his shoulder braces were hanging on either side of his legs.

Dad and the man shadow boxed while they bounced around the floor, aiming pretend blows at each other but not hitting their mark. There were Oooh and Aaah's from the audience when a fist shot out from either man, and Dad pranced around enjoying the performance he was putting on for them. His Irish grin never left his face.

Then the man jumped too far forward and caught Dad with a left to his chin. Then I let out a quick scream and became frightened for the man because I knew my father only too well; he wouldn't let him get away with that. The smile on Dad's face twitched in the corners and his eyes took on a steely glare. He lunged at the man with a swift right to the chest followed by a left uppercut to his chin, putting him on his backside in shock.

I knew it! I thought. *He shouldn't have done that to my dad.*

The audience was going crazy. Dad was getting accolades from everyone as they held his right hand in the air. He walked forward with a different smile now and stood before the man with his legs astride, his head on one side, and he held out his hand to the man on the carpet and hauled him up.

"Fair fight, fair fight," he was saying. They shook hands, put their arms around each other's shoulders, and everyone had a party. Dad had made another friend out of an enemy.

Dad helped in a local boxing club with the youth of the area and so his performance was merely an opportunity for him to show off his boxing skills. Plus being Irish, a good scrap was a necessity in his life. Nobody was ever seriously hurt and a singsong and a knees-up always followed.

We grew up never knowing what Saturday night would bring.

Love and fear created happy and frightening memories of our childhood, and the two extremes were entirely dependent upon our dad, whether he was drunk or sober. Dad, along with all the other men who had fought in the war, gathered in the pubs and drank to drown their memories and flashbacks of fighting. Mum managed the result of the beer drunkenness well but we discovered that whisky was fire water to Dad and he then behaved like a wounded bull. It wasn't a pretty sight and something that we kids feared. He never physically harmed us but we had to watch him fight our Mum and that harmed us mentally.

Because we were raised amongst other families like us, we never thought we were any different from any other family, but as adults, we can see our upbringing was different from most.

Carnforth Street was a hill with a street carved down the centre of it. The prefabricated houses on the left side were placed two abreast, rising two overlooking two as the hill rose from the main road. Our house was number two and the first on the left. On the right side of Carnforth Street, the houses faced the street. Each house had two bedrooms, one bathroom, one living room, and a kitchen, all mod cons.

Because the street housed the men that had fought in the war, we were raised hearing stories of war from all the neighbours, and the pain it inflicted and the damage it had left on the souls of men that had fought. The bombs that had been dropped on their wives and families and the people killed were spoken of regularly and never forgotten. Mister Fairhead was only one of the many men in our neighbourhood that had suffered shell shock. Allowances were made for all our neighbours because they had suffered in one way or another because of the war. Shell-shock was accepted because of the war, and some years later it was recognized properly as *Post Traumatic Stress Disorder* – PTSD. But in the years right after the war, our street was like any other street where most of the men suffered from the aftereffects of war in one way or another. We were one large family unit. Neighbours cared for and helped each other in any way they could.

Mum had many older sisters and was the recipient of their hand-me-downs of clothes, stockings, make-up, and shoes. This meant our house was the place other female neighbours called to be dressed when they were going somewhere special. It didn't matter if they weren't the same shoe size, they would jam their feet into Mums' shoes for the evening and, if Mum didn't have any stockings to lend them, she would stand them on a kitchen chair and carefully draw a line down the back of their legs to give the impression they were wearing seamed stockings.

If a neighbour was ill or finding themselves in financial hardship, the rest of the street fed the family until they were on their feet again. Summer evenings found everyone out in the street sitting on their front garden walls and chatting. On weekends, when it became dark, Mum and Dad would sometimes invite them all in around our living room while Dad played the piano and everyone sang. Because we had a piano we were classed as the 'posh' ones in the street.

Within the 'family unit', they would criticize a neighbour for one thing or another but when the chips were down for that person they still rallied around and helped.

Mrs Murphy was such a soul. She had no idea how to organize her family. She could not budget her money to make it last through the week and her house looked poor and bare. There were no curtains on Mrs Murphy's windows and she had one small old easy chair without cushions in her living room, and mattresses only on the bedroom floors. Many families wished they lived in these modern prefabricated houses. The local council rented these houses and someone had jealously reported this situation. Mrs Murphy was told if she didn't furnish her home and take care of it she would be evicted and a family that would appreciate it would be placed there. She was given four weeks to create a home.

The neighbours immediately rallied around; they dyed sheets and placed them as curtains on her windows. They scrubbed and cleaned and gave her pieces of furniture they didn't need anymore. The rag and bone man that called each week with his horse and cart was asked to find some half-decent furniture and some beds for them, which he did. When the housing authorities came four weeks later, they saw a neat tidy home and the Murphys were told the Council would inspect every three months after that, but for now, her family was allowed to stay. Every three months the neighbours cleaned Mrs Murphy's home for the housing inspection.

Mrs Murphy was a 'simple soul', my mother used to say. At the end of each day when the siren would blast out from the local shipbuilding yard to announce the end of the working day, the housewives would powder their faces and put clean aprons on and stand on the front steps with their children awaiting their man returning home from work. Because we were on a hill, the steps to each house were about five high. All the men worked in Cammell Lairds and would begin to walk home along Borough Road, all climbing the streets and disappearing inside their homes. They would file past the women on the steps of their homes and touch the tip of their caps and nod their heads in their direction as a sign of respect.

Mrs Murphy was a large round lady. She would stand on her steps along with the rest of the women in the street to welcome her man home. On this day, her youngest was crying and she lifted her onto her hip. As the men looked up to tip their caps, they began to click their tongues and smile, saying, "Hello there, luv!" one after the other. Mrs Murphy was acting coy, smiling, and saying words such as "Ooh, go on with ye! My fella will 'ave yer life if ee heard ye."

My father tipped his cap to Mrs Murphy and walked on to my mother and whispered in her ear. My mother immediately ran to Mrs Murphy, saying, "Ye frock, look at ye frock!" Mrs Murphy had lifted her child onto her hip but the child's foot had caught the hem of her dress and hitched it up, and Mrs Murphy was showing the world … she had no knickers on!

Opposite *The Happy Valley* pub at the bottom of the street, and across Borough Road, was The General Library with a bust of King George in bronze on its grounds. For the Hicks kids, this building was full of magic and wonder. We mention this building because reaching our seventh birthday was burned into our memories by all the Hicks kids as the day we joined the library. We would be playing in the street and on our birthday we would eagerly watch for Dad to turn the corner of the street from Borough Road, arriving home from work.

As he came into sight, we'd run squealing with excitement back into the house shouting, "Dad's nearly home, Mum!" She would grab the damp flannel that sat on the side of the kitchen sink and run it over our face. Our hair would be brushed and off we would go holding Dad's hand as he took each of us in turn, on our seventh birthday, over Borough Road to join the Birkenhead Library. Dad would have a copy of our birth certificate to prove we were seven years old that day. This was our birthday present.

Proudly he would speak to the librarian, saying, "My wee girl 'ere is seven today an' it is 'er birthday, and she'd like t'join the library please."

This was a rite of passage to the Hicks kids. With both Mum and Dad being avid readers and all their children then members of the library, our house was always full of books, and every one of us read the books that all of us had borrowed before they were returned.

Our parents always knew where to look for us – if not lying on the floor reading, we would be either playing in the street or in our local Birkenhead Park.

We had a small, enclosed back garden, and as a child, I would perform a concert all on my own and charge the kids in the street a halfpenny to come in and sit on the grass to watch me. They never did have a halfpenny so I would say they could have it on tick (drip payment!). I had heard the women in the neighbourhood using this expression; often when they wanted to buy something and didn't have the money they would say, 'I'll have to get it on tick.' So I thought that meant for free. 'Mister Umbrella' (Flanagan and Allen) was my favourite song as I could dance to that with Mum's umbrella.

The corrugated iron shed in our garden was Dad's work shed and was also used for coal. From time to time, it would house assorted items that were of no use to us anymore and would sit there ready to be disposed of. Dad had placed a chest of drawers in there that had peeling paint. One summer school holidays I decided it could be broken up and made into firewood. Mum was out for the day and I was minding Walter. Between us, we chopped this piece of furniture up and tied a string around small bundles which we placed in the old pram. Then Walter and I pushed it around the neighbourhood selling the bundles of wood for a half penny. We managed to sell the lot and were so pleased with ourselves. We stopped at the sweet shop on our way home and bought a penneth of sweets each and sat on our front steps eating them and waiting for Mum. When she arrived home, we proudly presented her with the money we had gathered, both of us smiling as I told her what we'd done.

"Oh, dear God, ye father will be beside himself as he was about to repaint it for our bedroom," she informed us. I do remember that was the first heavy smack of my bum from Dad. Walter wasn't smacked as he had been led astray by me!

Johnson, Walter, and Pauline

My relationship with Dad
1948 – 1956

Walter

I was a skinny but extremely healthy boy with thick wavy hair. Pauline had the same colour wavy hair and I judged how my hair looked by looking at my sister. Sometimes it looked wild because it grew up and out instead of down and Dad would cut it back with the small garden shears. I also quickly grew to be the same size as my sister Pauline and, during those years, people would sometimes think we were twins.

At the age of four, I figured out that the 'next' world my parents often referred to had to be on top of this one. My theory was confirmed one day when I looked up to see a galleon in full sail cruising smoothly along the top of the sky.

My imagination made me live in constant fear of ghosts; hence I was terrified of the dark. Ghosts were everywhere. They were the ghosts of people that had been killed by German bombs. With wide-eyed attention, I would eavesdrop as my parents talked of poor Mr Jones, who wouldn't go to the air raid shelter and was then killed when a bomb landed directly on his house. Or poor old Mrs Smith that was beheaded by a piece of flying glass.

When I wasn't thinking about ghosts or the world on top of this one, I was trying to figure out how I could get to America, or was it, Africa, at the time? I always got them mixed up. But there was no confusion about why I wanted to go there: I wanted to be a cowboy. In my imagination, the horse, the hat, the boots, and the gun would be provided for me upon arrival, and I would ride off, smiling happily, into the sunset – with The Lone Ranger tune playing in the background. Twenty-five years later, I did get to America but the customs people were not as welcoming as I thought they would be, way back, when I kneeled on the pavement drawing guns and horses with a piece of brick as a pencil.

When I was seven years old, the Queen paid a visit to Birkenhead. Along with all the other children, we lined Borough Road to await the Queen's motorcade of Rolls Royces. With my small flag, I excitedly jumped up and down and yelled as loud as the next child as the cars slowly made their way along the road where we were standing. Her Majesty waved in a strange circular motion that encouraged more waves and cheers and I was struck with awe when she looked directly at me. Pauline grabbed my hand when she'd gone by, saying the Queen looked directly at her as well. Bursting with excitement, we ran home and catapulted through the door of the prefab, yelling.

"I saw the Queen. I saw her! And she waved right at me."

"And what the fuck 'as she dun fer yer lately!" came a reply in a thick Belfast brogue.

I was stopped cold! I could not think of a thing that the Queen had done for me. Not lately anyway. *Why were we kids all lined up to wave and cheer for a Queen who doesn't do anything for anyone?* I could only stare at my father in wonder.

Our iron shed in the garden was one piece of corrugated iron in the shape of an arc. This was an ideal spot to climb onto on a balmy day and spit. The grooves in the corrugated iron kept the spit in a perfectly straight line as it ran down the sides of the shed to the ground. You had to be quick at spitting in two grooves at the same time so that they both had the same start, then you would see which one hit the ground first. I spent many happy hours racing spit! My only problem in playing this game was that the spit left white lines on the black corrugated iron.

Dad was proud of creating the best landscaped garden in the area. His free time was always spent in the garden. A wire mesh fence surrounded the garden and neighbours often stopped to talk to Dad through the fence while they admired his handiwork.

"It's the fuckin' spit 'ouse," he'd roar when he saw the white lines on his shed.

"When I tells them people where I lives thee say, Oh yeh! The' fuckin' spit 'ouse!"

Mum would immediately take my side!

"Oh yes!" she'd say. "Well I've heard people say it's the house of the drunken Irishman. The man that can't come home at night to his wife and kids because he must go to the bloody pub. Oh Yeah! I hear that he's a fine man all right, a very generous man, but I wouldn't know meself because he's always in the bloody pub!"

Dad was not the same when he'd been drinking and Mum was a nervous wreck because of it. We'd hear him coming home from the pub walking up the hill singing all the way.

"I'll take you home again Kathleen!
To where yer heart will feel no pain,
An where the trees are fresh and green,
I'll take you to your home Kathleen."

Timing his songs perfectly to end as he walked in the door. He always looked as though he was in a good mood when he first came home, but just seeing Mum, and merely knowing she wouldn't be happy about him drinking, he would turn suddenly into attack mode. They would fight – my mother's high-pitched anger against my father's deep and expressive Belfast accent. My mother's favourite line would be "I'll dance on your grave". I put it down to them both being a bit 'bomb happy' and always getting out of their way. I never felt in any personal danger but the shouting did get on my nerves.

Dad joined the army at the beginning of the war and served well for most of it as a motorcycle dispatch rider. When the call went out for volunteers for a new kind of force going under the name of Commando, Dad volunteered. Mum objected but Dad ignored her.

He did well in the advanced training and was made a sergeant and it was only over the latter year of the war that he saw that kind of action.

Dad was proud of his war record. Some nights after the pub and when I was a little older and not yet in bed, he would tell me his war stories, vividly describing different battles, guns blazing, airplanes dive bombing, tanks exploding. Then he would mention a name or two. Johnny Burgess and Frank Murphy were often co-heroes along with Dad in most of his stories. Then I would witness a change of expression on his face and his whole demeanour would be softened and he would be near tears. "Ah! deyze was good men," he would utter as he stared into the fire and nod his head, firstly, slowly up and down, then from side to side. Then he would look me straight in the eyes. I would stare back at him, mesmerized by the sudden change. His eyes were pleading with me to say or do something. I would want to say, "What can I do for ye, Dad?" but I never did.

We would sit for some time just staring into each other's eyes and I could see them moist with tears. Mum would interrupt us at about this time and I would be sent to bed. Mum would go to bed shortly after. I would then drift into my sleep to the sound of Dad going out to the much-abused spit shed for more coal to throw onto the already roaring fire.

*Christchurch School Borough Road
Football team. 1955/58 approx
Walter is back row first on the right.*

Dad's influence over our lives
1952 – 1956

Pauline

The area we lived in was called Merseyside, and Birkenhead was a town on the other side of the Mersey River from Liverpool. This part of England became known as the second capital of Ireland. The Irish Ferry boat docked in the port twice a week, bringing Irish immigrants that were escaping the IRA and looking for a better life. Most of them created their new life where they docked, on the banks of the Mersey, choosing either Liverpool or Birkenhead.

Drinking alcohol was the main pastime of many of the men in this area and so my father didn't stand out as being any different.

Dad was sober more than he was drunk, and he took an interest in all his children and spent time with us when he could. He had a passionate pride in his family, and his home, and all his possessions, which included us, were better than anybody else had and he made a point of telling people this often, especially when he was drunk.

The stories of his past were exaggerated more each time he told us, and his children sat and listened spellbound. He boomed them out to the ceiling or the walls while he talked as though he was speaking to a huge audience.

Dad played the piano often throughout the week as we, his kids, sang along with him. And he often amused us by singing and playing out of rhythm and tune – we would be rolling around the floor in fits of laughter. (As an adult, I did realize if you know how to play the piano properly, then to purposely play it badly was quite a clever thing to do.)

We would be convulsed with laughter at the noise he was making; but he, sombre-faced with a twinkle in his eye, would play on, then ask us what we were laughing at.

A boring job or situation could be turned into a fun-filled adventure. He taught us how to tend the garden and grow from seed. With one tuppenny packet of flower seeds, he would carefully count them into our hands. We had to give each seed a name then he would show us how to prepare the ground and plant them. We were told to water our seeds and talk to them every day. If they weren't watered and talked to, they wouldn't grow, he said. After school, instead of playing with the other kids in the neighbourhood, we could often be found lying on our stomachs, talking to a patch of earth.

Redecorating the house was great fun when we were each given a door to varnish and then shown how to draw a grain in it with a piece of cardboard cut like a comb. As the years went on, we must have improved in this art form but in the early days, those doors must have looked a mess, yet our dad showed our handy work to everyone that entered the house, boasting that any one of us could paint as good as that "Vangoof fella" (I do believe he was referring to Van Gough.)

He encouraged us to daydream. On a cold and rainy day when we couldn't play outside, he would lean on the windowsill with us as we stared waiting for the rain to stop, and he'd say,

"Now let us make dem black clouds go away; keep staring at dem and dey jus' disappears. Can ye see de sunshine? I can see it shinin' on de green grass. I can sees a field wid wee lambs in it, playing in de sunshine. What kin youse sees?"

Today it would be called visualization, but as children, it was our rainy-day game.

On some occasions, it would get us into trouble. In Christchurch School on Borough Road, we sat on the floor in the hall and listened to Mrs Maddocks, our music teacher, play the piano. Oh! She was my idol. I would sit and listen to the gentle, tinkly way she played the piano which was different from the heavy fingers of my dad. I dreamed of playing the piano like that myself one day in front of a large audience like the one I was sitting in. Approximately one hundred children. My daydreaming took over and although I had never had piano lessons at this stage in my life, I sat in my dream world staring at Mrs Maddocks, knowing she would soon be asking for someone to accompany her to play something beautiful on the piano. As soon as she did, I would raise my hand and she would announce me in front of all these people and I would be famous.

Mrs Maddocks stood up from the piano, walked to the front of the stage, and said 'something', which in my daydream was asking for this wonderful piano-playing person of whom she had heard. My hand shot up and she said my name. Excitement engulfed me as I uncurled my legs from my squatting position on the floor. I climbed over all the other children and walked with my back straight and my curls bouncing on my head, down the aisle left between the children and onto the stage. With a smile that stretched from ear to ear, I stood beside Mrs Maddocks looking down on all the children and I felt ten feet tall.

"Yes, Pauline?" said Mrs Maddocks with half a smile.

I looked up at her confused *What did she mean by 'Yes? I've come to play the piano with her.*

"Well, do you know the answer to my question?" she asked.

"What question?" I answered. I didn't know what she was talking about.

"You've been daydreaming again, Pauline, haven't you?" she said crossly. "Now go and sit down and pay attention."

This was my earliest memory of one of my most embarrassing

moments. My face was burning and I wanted to cry as I had to walk off the stage, back down the stairs, and pick my way through the crossed legs of the audience as they were giggling and laughing at me. But in the morning break from lessons when we all went into the play yard and the other kids were pointing and laughing at me, Peter Edbrook stood before me struggling to say something. He was one of the boys in my class and I had always liked Peter, but now I was feeling weepy as I thought that he too would laugh at me. He stared into my eyes, said nothing about my embarrassment, but leaned into me and gave me my first kiss. My embarrassment was over! I was in love!

Dad worked as a 'spider man', which was a name they gave to steel erectors on Birkenhead Docks. He boasted that he could walk across a four-inch beam suspended seventy feet in the air, without a nerve in his body. We believed him. Cammell Lairds, the company he worked for on the docks, built a lot of famous ships, and on their launching, he would take us to witness the ships that 'he' had built, and as kids, we believed he had done it single-handedly. He wanted us to be proud of him, and for a lot of things we were. The times we didn't boast about were his drunken bouts of rage, and the violent arguments with my mother after his drinking whisky, which we discovered, was fire water to him. On occasions, Mum ran into our bedroom to get away from him but he burst through the door, roaring abuse at her. We huddled together in fear in the corner of the double bed that we children shared. He never did hurt us but this scene would make us terrified. We would want to cry but we were too frightened to make a noise or he might notice us. Our hearts hammered away in our chests and we held onto each other for comfort. Our mother would be dragged from our room and the door slammed and we could hear her being physically knocked around the living room.

As children, we had been born with the Irish passion for life but it was occasionally suffocated in our young bodies, never knowing if the time was now to show our enthusiasm or to shut up.

We were never short of home comforts, my mother saw to that; she was an excellent manager with money and supplemented the household income by doing cleaning jobs. She was a good mother and sat in with us kids every night. She wasn't one to go to the pub as she only drank alcohol for an occasion. I remember when we were older that she began to have a movie night out with her sister from time to time and some years later when we were all grown, she began frequenting the Bingo halls with my Aunt Winnie. She never spoke to anyone about the abuse she suffered – she had her pride – and we all knew not to talk to anyone about Dad's drunken rages. She could only hold her head up high if she thought no one knew. Consequently, only a rare few people were aware of the life she led. Some were critical of her, not knowing the life she led behind closed doors with my father. People would see this clever, funny little Irish man and love his company but couldn't understand why his wife had such a poker face at times.

Dad mellowed as he got older and stopped being argumentative in drink, but he never stopped drinking. The two extremes of emotion that we children endured because of Dad's personality made it difficult because we really loved someone we also feared. He would turn in his grave if he thought he had harmed us in any way because he loved us all passionately. But Walter and I were overly sensitive and were emotionally harmed and it affected our entire lives.

In 1952, we had a new baby born into our family, a beautiful baby boy. He was named Johnson. Personally, this baby boy was mine. Walter was four now and didn't always want me to baby him. At the age of seven, I felt quite grown up as I shared Johnson's care. I learned how to change his nappies, bathe him, feed him, and dress him. I would place him in his pram and walk around the neighbourhood with him, stopping and talking to all the neighbours and showing him off. I was so proud of our new baby; he was the most beautiful child in the world. I would sit for hours teaching him to walk and talk. At the end of my school day, I would run home to spend some time with him, singing him songs, as he clapped his hands, letting me know he loved my singing. Nobody else was allowed to put Johnson to bed; I made it my sole responsibility to dress him in his night clothes, feed him his last bottle, then quietly sing and rock him until he was asleep. Oh, I did love that time with him.

While he was new-born he slept in his cot in Mum and Dad's room but as he grew, he was placed to sleep in my room with me and the other kids. My life was complete again now that I had another baby to care for. Mum and Dad told everybody I was a born mother.

We were growing like weeds and our sleeping arrangements were becoming extremely cramped. Not long after Johnson was born, Babs went to live with our Aunt Flo, Uncle Bill, and cousins Pat and William on Leinster Street in the North end of Birkenhead.

Walter playing on the bombed fields – approx. 1958/1961

Walk in the Park
1952.

Walter

I can't remember how old I was but I do remember the night that Dad came home worse than he had ever been after his drinking. He didn't sing on his way home that night and there was no warning when suddenly he stumbled in through the door. It must have been a Friday or Saturday because Pauline and I were still in the living room. By the wild look on his face, we knew it was time for us to go to bed. However, there was no escaping the noise. I did my best to tune it out but Dad's angry powerful voice seemed to vibrate around the house.

    I hear the front door slam and I know that Mum has run out of the house because all I can hear is Dad cussing and roaring about how he is a fuckin' slave. I'm glad Mum has gone. Now there will be some peace and maybe Dad will fall asleep, then in a little while she'll come back. I hear my sister whimpering and saying quietly *Mum, Mum, Mum,* but I tune it out, and I toss and turn until I fall asleep. I'm in the middle of a dream where I'm paddling along a wide river. I decide to turn around; I want to go back upstream but the current is too strong. I'm pushing my oars into the water for all I am worth but I'm still going downstream when Mum wakes me up.

    I see Pauline standing by the bedroom door. She's dressed in her outdoor clothes and still quietly crying but I can tell that she's trying to act brave. I rub my eyes and complain about being woken.

"Never mind that," Mum whispers. "Just get out of bed and be quiet."

She dresses me and takes me by the hand and we all walk through the living room where Dad is passed out in a chair. His mouth is open and I'm worrying that an earwig might crawl into it. I remember Dad's warning about earwigs *If they get in your ear then your ear will wiggle for the rest of your life.* But having one in your mouth and swallowing it is a far scarier thought than having a constant wiggling of the ear.

Mum walks us quietly past him with her finger over her lips, "shhh!!," showing but not saying, then we were out the door. Johnson was in the pram at the bottom of the steps. Mum tells us to hold the handle with her and help her push it up the hill, but I'm soon exhausted. I want to go back to my bed.

"Where are we going? "I ask.

"We're going to your Aunty Flo, that's all you need to know." Her voice sounded determined.

My sister walks holding the handle, I can hear a little sob now and then, but I'm scared to offer her any sympathy; if she breaks down and starts crying for real I wouldn't know how to manage it. I might even start crying myself. We get to the top of the hill and walk on for ages until we come to Birkenhead Park gates. I am surprised that the gates are open because they usually shut them before it gets dark, and it's very dark now. We pass through them and soon we are in the park and there are no lights at all. It is pitch black and it's incredibly quiet. I hang onto the pram and do my best to fight off the sleep. My sister isn't crying anymore, not even a sob. I can barely make her out as she holds the other side of the pram. Mum pushes on and the wheels of the pram squeak at regular intervals. There is no moon, no stars, just blackness, and the squeaking of the pram wheels.

"Mum, I'm scared," I hear my sister say."

"Hush now, there's nothing to be scared about," says Mum.

I am glad to hear her say that because I'm at the point of being terrified. But I believe in what Mum says, so I push back the fear and hold onto the pram with a white-knuckle grip. I walk on and try to be brave. I am now consumed in fear. But Mum is still pushing the pram. I can't see her; the pram is moving so I assume that she is pushing it. If Mum is there then I'll be all right. I think! I listen to try to hear her breathing, but the terror has got me and it's all I can do to just plant one foot in front of the other. The walk goes on forever, in the stillness, in the silence, placing one foot in front of the other and going further into blackness, a determined Mum, a baby, and two terrified kids. We plod on until behind a tree I glimpse a light. Then there are more lights, and soon I can see my sister and my Mum, then we come to the park gates, and they are closed!

Mum stops at the gates. I hang onto the pram and my sister starts crying for real now; she is really letting it out and I'm struggling to hold back my tears. I fight back the urge to cry, then I fight back the fear that we're going to be in this dark place all night. Then I look at Mum and I see in her face that she is still determined to go on. I take courage from her and I try to act determined too. Luckily, the gatekeeper hears my sister crying and comes out and opens the gates to let us out into Mallaby Street. Mum pushes on with us down Laird Street which is not pitch black now and has road lights, and on into my Aunt Flo's house and safety!

A few days later, my Mum takes us for a walk and we see Dad standing on a corner. He walks over to us and asks Mum if she will take him back. She smiles. He looks at Pauline and asks her if she will take him back. Pauline smiles. Then Dad smiles and hugs her. Then he asks me if I will take him back and I say no. Dad's smile turns into a frown and I can see that I have hurt him. I'm sorry that I've hurt him but I still don't want him back. It is the fighting that I don't want. I want my dad. I want his stories and his funny ways, but I can't stand any more of the fighting. I want to tell him how I feel but he's already turned away and he's now looking at Mum. Mum tells him to take no notice of me, that I am a bit confused owing to spending a few nights at Flo's house.

I glare at her. I want to know where the determination went. I want to know how she can take him back after all the things she and her sisters have been saying about him over the last few days. But I don't say a word. I place my gaze on a crack in the pavement and I feel my heart sink. We all go back to Aunt Flo's house and pack the pram with the same stuff that we left with. We put Johnson back in the pram as well and all walk back through the park again to the prefab.

The next Friday night they're at it again. Dad's deep Irish brogue and Mum's high-pitched anger. I feel like my insides are shrinking when I hear him "Yer've even turned me own son against me." I want to get out of bed and tell him that I haven't turned against him. I want to tell him that I love him, but boys can't say that, they can say they love dogs or football teams but anything else is considered to be sissy, so I just cover my ears with the pillow and try to soothe Pauline when she begins to cry.

The walk through the park was never repeated and, though I was younger than Pauline, it became clear that she would hug me and Johnson close, attempting to comfort us but needing solace herself for the fear she felt every time Dad came home from drinking.

Birkenhead Park

Birkenhead North General Information 1957-1966

Johnson was the fourth child to be born into the Hicks family, and so the detached two-bedroom prefabricated house was now too small for them all. Up until Babs left to live with their Aunty Flo, all four children had slept in a double bed in one room. To begin the night, the two girls were at one end of the bed and the two boys at the other. As soon as the light was switched off, Babs would take her position on one-third of the bed and Pauline and the boys nested together at the other end. This was how they liked to sleep, arms and legs entangled. The girls and the boys now had to be separated, and so a three-bedroom house was found. The two boys slept in one room and the two girls in another which meant bringing Babs back from Aunty Flo's to her family home. Pauline and her little brothers couldn't cuddle each night now and that was something that took some time for them all to come to terms with, especially Pauline.

Though the house had an extra bedroom, the living areas were smaller than the prefab. The world they had all become familiar with was about to change drastically. More than anything else they didn't want to leave the library behind, but they were assured there would be one near where they were going to live.

The brick terraced house had a front garden the width of the house and perhaps three meters long with a small fence separating it from the pavement. The back garden was a lot bigger and was surrounded by a high wooden fence. It was in the North End of Birkenhead. Corporation Road was one of the seven roads circling St. James' church.

The following historical information was taken from a small book written by Bill Houldin called *Up Our Lobby*.

> This area had become famous in the late 1800s for a set of buildings called the Dock Cottages. They had been situated at the nearest end of Ilchester Road to the church.
>
> The Birkenhead Dock Company, finding they needed accommodation for their numerous workers, decided in their wisdom, to build the first block of flats in England. This was a new concept then and the whole country looked on with interest to see if this idea would work and how it would affect the lives of the average working-class family. The name 'Dock Cottages,' conjures up the wrong picture of what were huge concrete blocks of one-room flats standing four high surrounding a concrete central community recreation area. These addresses were even Block One, block Two, etc. It resembled one of the old English Asylums.
>
> The Dock Cottages housed over one thousand people and after ninety years they eventually were demolished in 1940 and Ilchester Square, again another block of flats but more rooms to each flat, and modern facilities were erected.
>
> Once again, more than one thousand people were herded together to share family life. It created closeness unheard of anywhere else. If children fell over or hurt themselves they would run to any Mum to be cleaned up and kissed better. The centre of the blocks of flats, the concrete area, always had sports of some description being played there.
>
> It was known as a tough area, but these people

wouldn't see one of their own kind 'down and out.' Everybody supported each other and behind their tough exterior was a big fat heart.

Though the way of life in the flats did not create comfortable living, it did create two generations of excellent sportspeople, some of them famous and placing their names in the archives of English history.

Their names were bandied around these parts because they were neighbours and were classed as part of our extended family.

Dixie Dean, the famous footballer, played for Everton and England.

Wally Thom, British, and Empire welterweight boxing champion.

The Sutton brothers, Bill and Norman, golfers at the West Cheshire Artisans, Norman becoming World Champion in 1958.

The area also produced many successful caddies to the rich and famous golfers and stories of lives we could only imagine were spread throughout the community from the many pubs in the area where the men gathered regularly.

It became clear soon after moving into this house that those living on the roads surrounding Ilchester Square were also part of this community.

Opposite the house on Corporation Road was a high brick wall surrounding a huge building called 'The Prince Albert Memorial Industrial School.' The building was designed to accommodate one hundred boys. Those admitted were deemed to need care or they had been committed for some misdemeanour. The school had been closed since 1924 and now sat idle and empty. It still didn't stop their Mum from threatening them with it.

"If you don't behave yourself, I'll put you in the naughty boys' home!" It was always just a huge brick wall to the Hicks kids.

The transition from Junior to Senior school 1957 – 1962

Walter

Johnson started his schooling right away at Laird Street School when he was five. I was only nine years of age when we moved house and so I stayed at Christchurch school and was given four pence every day to catch the bus. I would get on the double-decker bus and always went upstairs hoping to get the front seat. Then the bus conductor would come around banging her bag with the money in it. Meanwhile, I'm looking out the window like I've been on the bus for the last half hour. "Tickets please," she says, banging her money bag more. I glance towards her and she is staring right at me.

"A tuppeny," I say.

"A tuppeny what?" she answers.

"A tuppeny ticket"

"A tuppeny ticket what?"

I am baffled, I feel myself blushing as the other people on the bus look at us.

"A tuppeny ticket to the General Library" I offer.

"A tuppeny ticket to the General Library what?" she says again – now everyone is looking at me wondering what I will respond with this time.

"A tuppenny ticket to the General Library and …." I crease my forehead wondering what this conductor wants out of me. I stare at her and think, *just take the two pennies, and give me the ticket!*

"A tuppeny PLEASE!" she states loudly like she's just defeated this kid and is looking for praise from all on the bus.

"A tuppeny please," I mutter, my face flushed with embarrassment. She then rings out the ticket and wanders on down the bus banging her money bag and saying.

"Tickets please"

At the end of a boring Friday at school, my teacher tells the class that we'll be having the eleven-plus exam first thing Monday morning, so we should all get to bed early on Sunday night and be ready for it. *The eleven-plus! What is so difficult about that? Ask me to add eleven to any number under the sun and I'll solve it for you in a moment.* However, on Monday morning I could only stare at the test paper. I failed the eleven-plus exam but I didn't care, in a few weeks I would be out of this school where they made us wear ties and feel embarrassed about the holes in our socks, and from now on I wouldn't have to ride the bus to school anymore. I had already found new friends with the boys living near our house so I wanted to go to the same school as they were going to. Life was great. Then came the holidays. We had six weeks off school and good riddance to stuck-up Mrs Moss and the stuck-up headmaster, Mr Lockyer, who was always telling the boys to use only water on our hair – Corporation hair oil he called it every flippin' morning in assembly and was the only one who laughed at his words. *Ah! I won't have to listen to that ever again!*

When we moved into Corporation Road, and over the two years before, I joined my secondary school, I became acquainted with the kids in the North End. One of my new friends was Alan Cunningham. We developed an illegal get-rich-quick scheme. We would stuff cardboard up the chute of telephone boxes where the money comes out if the call doesn't go through, and periodically we gathered our ill-gotten gains. Johnson would sometimes join us and his small hands were just the right size to push the cardboard back up the chute. We scraped the penny arcade machines in the same way in New Brighton and robbed empty bottles from the backyard of a shop on Laird Street then take the bottles back to the same shop for refund money. The bottle idea was mine but I wasn't savvy enough in petty crime to think it through and take the bottles back to a different shop after we had robbed them. We got caught on that caper though. The shop owner no sooner put the empty bottles in his backyard than we were over the wall again and then back into the front door looking innocent and with our hands out for the refund money. The police let us off with a warning. They had Dad take me and Johnson to the Laird Street police station, where the chief inspector told us off. Although our fear was palpable, I'm sure I heard laughter as we were leaving.

Grange Secondary Modern School was the name of my new school but there was nothing modern about it. It was on Tollemache Road in Birkenhead and was known to everyone as Tolly. I'm shaking the sleep out of my eyes and getting ready for my first day. I have a new pair of jeans and new socks but I still have a few grey shirts left from the school uniform of Christchurch so Mum thinks I'll be all right in one of them. Pauline is already going to her new school and is eating her cereal. She's wearing the uniform for Park High School for Girls. I sense something in the fact that she is still going to a school where they wear uniforms and I am not! I found out that the eleven-plus exam was to see what kind of school we were to attend after we passed the age of eleven. Pauline was obviously still worth educating, and equally as obvious I wasn't! But I didn't care. My ambition went no further than being a labourer on a building site, and that seemed to me like it was a grand thing to be. *Who needs education?* I'm happy and I'm expecting this new school to be a breeze.

Still, I'm too nervous to eat anything, so I say tarah to them all and set off on my mile walk to Tolly. Lenny, my friend, is waiting on the corner of the road for me. He is smoking a cigarette and spitting every few seconds.

"Ow the fuck are ye?" he enquires.

"Fuckin' great," I answer. I had already learned that cussing in this area is a verbal badge showing you belong and you're not a sissy.

I take a glance at the attire that Lenny is wearing for his first day at his new school. His shirt is a dirty white with a few brown stains around the collar due to the margarine he uses to slick his hair back. His jeans are ragged and have holes in them and the soles of his shoes flop up and down when he walks. Lenny is the only protestant kid in our gang that is starting school with me at Tolly. Most of the other kids I know are Catholics and they are all going to the other Secondary Modern waste of time! The only difference is they get to learn a bit about religion. Or that is what I think. *Glad it's not me!*

"Yer gunna av to do some tin about that fuckin stutter, mate," he says. "They'll fuckin' murder ye for doin' dat in dis school."

I am shocked! It hadn't even occurred to me! *Did I stutter?*

My attempt at composure vanishes and the butterflies in my stomach turn into fear. Why hadn't anyone told me before now that I stutter? My heart races, and I envision myself as being the brunt of all the school bullies. Me! A stutterer!

I try to take courage from Lenny. He is walking along like it's another day of the year. He is spitting off the end of his tongue like he has been doing it since he was born. It occurs to me that it is not an act, he really is like that. His clothes no longer matter, and I swear that I will never be critical of anyone ever again because of what they wear. I would change clothes with him in a second if I could be him for this day and he be me.

We got to school early so we can be thrown into the bushes before all the other new kids arrive. It was a school ritual we had been advised of by the kids in the neighbourhood. The older kids were waiting for us, and we laughed like good sports as they pick us up by our hands and feet, and on the count of three, we fly off into a new episode in our lives.

We're enjoying the sight of the other new boys being thrown around when suddenly a whistle is blown. Most of the boys stand like they are frozen stiff. The new boys don't know that we are supposed to stop immediately at the sound of the whistle, and I'm still wandering around and spitting as best I can.

"You, boy!"

I turn towards the sound and see that he's shouting at me!

"What is your name, boy?"

All I can think of is that I mustn't stutter. The whole bloody school is watching and if I stutter now I'll be known all over as a stutterer. I try to say my name but nothing will come out.

"The cat got your tongue, boyo?" the teacher says.

The other new kids have stopped moving by now and the whole school playground is still; it is silent. All eyes are on me and the teacher. He strides toward me and then starts to twist my ear.

"I said, what is your name?"

The ear twisting helps. I can pretend that the grimace on my face is because of the pain from the ear twisting and has nothing to do with the effort I have to summon and force out my name.

"Hicks," I eventually manage to say.

"Hicks what?"

"Walter Hicks."

"Walter Hicks what?"

"Walter Hicks please," I offer.

"Walter Hicks please what?" he says – I'm dumbfounded again.

"Walter Hicks, please let go of my ear."

The teacher laughs and lets go of my ear.

"Sir," he says and looks around as he raises his voice. "You will all call me sir."

"Yes, sir," I say.

He gets hold of my ear again and twists it.

"Walter Hicks, sir," I say, catching on.

He lets go of my ear and blows his whistle. The older boys move. After a second or two, or more, according to nerve and mental agility, the new kids move too.

Lenny is smiling at me. "Fuck 'im," he says. (That was true support from a mate.)

Then we are all jostling to get in the door and fight our way up the stairs. Suddenly I am pushed against the side wall by an older boy and he is right in my face.

"I know about you," he says, "You're fuckin' Irish an' we don't want the fuckin' Irish here. They hate the Queen and we love the fuckin' Queen. Get back to the fuckin' bog, ye ignorant Mick!"

I am so shocked that I forget that I stutter.

"You love the Queen?" I say incredulously.

"Yes, we love her."

"Why?"

For a split second, I'm sure he looks confused, but the discussion is ended by the mass of boys as they push into us.

"I'll get you!" he threatens into my face.

I secretly thank him. He's shocked me back to my old self and I'm not feeling the fear in my stomach anymore. I can take being bullied because I am Irish; I can live with that, but to be bullied because I stuttered! Ahh, that's the end of the world, or at least it would have been as far as my eleven-year-old ego was concerned.

We congregate in the big hall. New boys to the front, older boys to the back with the oldest boys standing smugly in the rear. No one is saying a word. The teachers are lined up along the sides of the hall watching out for mischief.

"Good morning, boys."

No answer came from the boys.

He's standing on a stage and he's all decked out in a black hat and gown like they wear at fancy public schools.

"I'm sure we'd like to give our new boys a warm welcome."

Total silence

"But first of all, we'll say our morning prayers."

He starts the 'our father' and everyone joins in until the end when there's a loud "Amen."

There's a piano on the stage with a woman who looks like she's been poured into a mould, and sits staring at the headmaster, hands hovering over the right keys and ready to play. He looks her way and nods and she hits a note and the teachers and returning students all start singing.

And did those feet in ancient time
Walk upon England's mountain green?
And was the holy Lamb of God
On England's pleasant pastures seen?
And did the countenance divine
Shine forth upon our clouded hills?
And was Jerusalem builded here
Among those dark satanic mills?
Bring me my bow of burning gold!
Bring me my arrows of desire!
Bring me my spear! O clouds, unfold!
Bring me my chariot of fire!
I will not cease from mental fight,
Nor shall my sword sleep in my hand,
Till we have built Jerusalem
In England's green and pleasant land.

WOW!

All male voices singing with power in a way I had never heard that song sung before!

I'm a gonna!! I'm completely spaced out.

The first morning's service is over before I realize it's even begun and the older boys are now being dismissed. Soon only a few teachers and the new boys remain in the hall.

"Listen for your names," a big man is shouting.

"When I call out your name you will say "Here,"; is that understood?"

The boys all nod and act like they understood.

"I can't hear you!" The big man is holding his ear and bending his head as he's trying to catch a tiny sound.

There's a sound of mumbling and the odd "Yes."

"Okay," he says. "These boys will be in form A."

He reads a list of about forty names and all the boys are taken away by a teacher. Then the man reads out the names of form B. They are then taken away by another teacher.

I've heard enough about the school to know that form A is for the brightest boys. These are the kids who knew what the eleven plus was and who even tried to pass it but failed by only a small margin. Form B is for the next brightest, they failed the eleven-plus by a distinct margin but showed some intellectual ability. Form C is the first level of the no-hope-whatsoever class and I'm getting a bit worried now because I was hoping that I would at least get into Form B. The big man is now reading out the names for Form C and I feel relief sweep through me as he calls out my name. *Could have been worse!*

Our assigned teacher is a big, rosy-faced man who smiles when he introduces himself to us. He then does a swift change of face and tells us to stand in two lines. He goes down the lines scowling with displeasure, then smiles again like he's enjoying a private joke.

"I want no talking, and I want you to march to your classroom in good order. When I say left, I mean that you should start walking with your left foot. When I say right it means that your right foot should follow your left foot. Have I made myself clear?" he shouts.

Silence!

"Have I made myself clear!" He's getting red in the face.

A mumbling of "yes" comes from the boys.

"By the right, quick march!" he yells. "Right left, right left, right left …" and we all stumble into each other and Percy Potman falls over and starts crying.

These madmen that say we must call them sir seem determined to teach us something. They drill us like we are recruits in the army; they tell us where to sit and warn us of the consequences if we wreck the desks. Each desk has an ink pot in it and there's a stick with a pen nib on the end of it. The master writes a timetable on the chalkboard that tells us what classes we'll be having each day.

"At the end of each class, you are to form two lines in the hall until the teacher of that class comes for you. And if anyone falls over again, he's in for six of the best on his arse." I glance at Percy; he looks like he's going to start crying again.

Finally, they let us out for a break. I find Lenny. He tells me that he's in Form E. I want to ask him if there's a Form F, but I don't. He doesn't say much. He flips spit off the end of his tongue and walks around with his hands in his pockets, his shoes flap as they did earlier on that morning, and he still looks like the world can kiss his arse, but now I don't want to change places with him. Being put in Form C in a school for failures is bad enough. I think to myself that Lenny doesn't even know that he took the eleven-plus. I imagine that, maybe, Lenny is ashamed of being in class 'E.'

"If that lad had done that to me like 'ee did te you I'd 'ave stuck the 'ead on 'im," he says.

Now I think that Lenny is ashamed of me! I'm sure he thinks that I acted like a coward when the bully pinned me to the side of the corridor. I know that Lenny means what he says and I have no doubt at all that he would have head-butted the bully into oblivion if it was him being pinned to a wall.

I stop walking but Lenny walks on. He's calm. He's collected. He's a man in a boy's body. He brings up a big green gob of spit from his nose and spits it on the playground.

I feel no shame. The bully didn't scare me. I look around and some kids are playing football. I ask them if I can join in but there's no response; they are into the game; so, I just start playing with them and soon I hear one of them say, "He's good!"

Learning to live in the North End and now adjusting to my secondary school was a total shock to the psyche. Daily there was something new to absorb and at times it was overwhelming. And shortly after starting Tolly, Dad produced another major learning curve. It was a Saturday and I had walked into the kitchen for my dinner (which is lunch in today's vernacular) when Dad puts a hand on my shoulder and says that we're going for a walk. We walk in silence until we get to the duck pond in the park, then he looks me in the eyes. "Your Mum thinks it's time I tell yer the facts of life," he says.

I feel embarrassed as I've already heard a lot about that in the schoolyard and I don't want to hear it from Dad. I'm hoping I'm hiding my embarrassment well until I realize that my face is on fire.

"Now then," he says "I was raised on a farm so my Dah never had to tell me the facts of life so I've got nothing to go by. I can see that you're a wee bit embarrassed too so I'll try to make it short and simple." Dad then used animals as he explained to me the reproductive action necessary to make babies. I wasn't listening properly, my face burned as I looked at the ground and moved ant hills around with my shoe. Thankfully, I did hear his final statement:

"And that's what you do to make babies. Now, do you have any questions?"

"Does the Queen do that too?" I ask.

"Aye, of course she does; everyone does it. I have it on good authority that she even takes a good crap in the morning too."

"Does she wipe her own bum?" I ask in all seriousness.

"I hardly think she'd have her butler do that," Dad says.

I sit staring at him, I can't imagine it! but if Dad says so then it must be true.

"Well, that's that then," says Dad.

We smell the clean fresh air and feel the soft breeze as we watch the ducks floating aimlessly around the pond. A pair of ducks splash down and leave a trail on the water as they skid to a halt. Suddenly a black mongrel bounds past us and jumps into the pond. The ducks all paddle away quacking furiously. The dog does a complete circle of the pond and then comes out right beside us to shake himself dry. We jump away from him and start laughing. The dog is laughing too. His tongue is out; his tail is wagging and his eyes are full of joy. We both pat him and tell him that he's a good dog. Then we hear a man's voice.

"Here, boy; come, Rover."

Rover bounces out of our life just as suddenly as he came into it. As the ducks settle down again I realize that I like being in the park with my Dad, however, I don't want to talk about sex and the Queen's toilet habits anymore, so I scramble for something to say to change the subject.

"Danny Kelly said that his Dad got a medal in the war," I say.

"Aye, now is that right?"

"He said his Dad was in the navy and that when he saw a torpedo coming towards the ship his Dad dived in the water and pushed the torpedo away from the ship and saved everyone's lives."

Dad's got a grin on his face. "Ah, yes," he says "Let me tell you another fact of life. Sex and fighting are two subjects in life that men usually lie about. I think that's what they mean when they say that all's fair in love and war."

"Do you have any medals, Dad?" I ask.

His smile fades from his face. "I had some."

"Where are they?"

"I threw them away."

A man at the other end of the pond is about to throw a stone into the water and we both watch as the stone arcs down and then splashes, then we watch the ripples as they grow wider.

"It was a rare man that became a hero," Dad says, "but there weren't many men that I'd call a coward either."

I can see that he's getting that distant look that he gets when he's staring at the fire in the hearth.

"When the shells and the bullets came flying at us for the first time there wasn't one of us that didn't piss in our pants. Most of the men couldn't pull the trigger to save their lives and if they did pull the trigger, they aimed high so as not to hit anyone. It's not easy to kill another man, no, it's not as easy as they make it out to be in the pictures. Not at all."

"Did you aim high?" I ask him.

"Not at first," he says, "but towards the end, when the writing was on the wall and it was all over bar the shouting, I shot wide and high. The Germans knew it was over and they were ready to surrender. They just wanted to fire a few rounds to make it look good. They'd fight to the death against the Russians, but they were ready to surrender to us and the Yanks."

I glance up at him and I see that his eyes are full of tears so I quickly look away.

He sighs. "It was the last firefight of the war. I knew we were only fighting a group of boys so I told the men not to kill them. I knew that we could scare them half to death with a few well-placed grenades. Sure enough, they quickly surrendered. At least most of them did. But as we advanced to take them prisoner a few that were still hidden opened on us. That's when Johnny and Frank got it."

"Johnny and Frank were killed?"

"Aye."

"So, you think that you made the wrong decision because your mates got killed?"

"Aye, but then again, it seemed like the right decision at the time. The regular German soldiers wouldn't pull that kind of stuff."

I now understand why he stares into the fire when he's drunk. I feel sorry for him but I know better than to let him know it.

"Did you ever kill anyone?"

"I shot and saw them falling, but it could have been anyone that killed them. Ah, dey was just the same kind of daft bastards that we were. I'm sure we'd have all gotten along fine in the pub." He laughs like he's amazed at his own stupidity.

"Why did you do it?" I ask. "Why did you fight for the Queen?"

My question ignited his anger. "I didn't fight for the Queen. I fought for you and the likes of you. I fought for your mum and your brother and sisters. Ah, what t'e fuck, I also did it because I didn't want to be called a coward. Aye, that's about the truth of the matter. But when you get in a battle you fight for yer mates. Fer fuck sake, yer mates are all you have in that situation. T'e hell wid the flag; yer fight fer yer mates."

"War sounds scary," I say.

"Aye, it is," he says now without anger, "but fear is a funny thing. It's not so bad when you put someone before yerself. It wasn't my own death that scares me, I'll tell ye that. Sometimes I thought I'd be better off dead! No, it was the fear that we'd screw up and be the cause of one of our mates copping it. That's what scared us."

I pick up a stone and I'm about to throw it into the pond, but he stops me.

"Cum on," he says. "Leave the ducks in peace. It's time to go."

We walk back along the same route that we came, in the same silence, and then when he comes to the pub.

"I'm just goin in for a quick one. You go on home."

I stand and watch as he walks into the pub. I know that I won't see him again that day. He'll stagger in after ten-thirty when the pubs shut and then he and Mum will go at it again. She'll say that she'll dance on his grave and he'll roar about how he's a fuckin slave.

Then I think about the men in battle that aimed high, and I wonder why I never got told about it before now. I decide that I am going to ask my history teacher about it. There must be a lot of men still alive because of the ones that did aim high. I struggle but cannot grasp the concept that has come into my head. Would it be better in a war to kill or not to kill?

Then the door to the pub opens and Dad is waving his arm in the general direction of our house. He's smiling like he's just heard a great joke and he's shouting, "Go home!"

I realize that my eyes haven't left the pub door since he went in it. I smile at him and give a quick wave. Then, when he goes back inside, I walk back to the duck pond. I like the ducks. What a life! They just swim around the pond all day. They have the odd argument with another duck then one will chase the other and they'll fly around for a bit, then for some unseen reason, they'll both flap their wings furiously like getting rid of the upset, and then go back to paddling around in the pond.

I feel proud of my Dad for not wanting to kill the boy soldiers. His decision saved their lives. Now the boys would be grown up and have children of their own, and then their children would grow up and have more children, and on and on it would go, some of them might be doctors, and doctors save other people's lives, and all those future lives affected, and all because my dad decided not to kill those boys in the war.

But what of Johnny and Frank? No children will come from them. Was it Dads' fault they died? I think not. The blame must go to the people that started the war! Then, as my thoughts go deeper, I see that the soldier that pulls the trigger that fires a bullet that takes a life is just the last chain of events in an extensive line of causes and effects. My mind struggles as the complexity of the concept comes into my view. The impossibility of assigning guilt is imprinted in my mind forever, and I can see clearly that the last cause of an effect, like the man that pulls the trigger, shouldn't be the sole bearer of all the guilt.

My mind then turns to another confusing concept, a concept that baffles me and shuts down my powers of reasoning even faster than that of cause and effect. I think about the Queen having sex. I try to imagine Prince Philip and the Queen doing what Dad's just told me! How can it be, that one who waves as she does, and holds herself as she does, how could it be possible that she does what the rest of us do to make babies? Try as I can, I cannot imagine the Queen in that context.

But it's all been too much for one day and my mind completely shuts down. So, I sit in perfect silence for a few minutes and just watch the ducks floating around. They have a pretty good life. Then I think that an egg butty would be nice, so I decided to go home.

Walter age approx. 13

Johnson age approx. 9

Tollemache School
1959 – through 1960s

Walter

I was surprised to find out that as far as our education went Tollemache School meant to give it a try. They certainly gave us enough subjects. We had the usual English and math as well as history and geography. We also had art classes, music classes, gym classes, and science classes along with real lab experiments, a woodworking class where they started us off straight away on making our own table. They even gave us a test to see if we were in the right class and as a result, I was moved up to class B.

I was happy at this level. The boys in the A stream didn't seem to have the requirements to be Huckleberry Finn. They all wore nice clothes, and overall, they were taking it all a bit too seriously. I was sure that if I went up to the A stream then most of them would see me as Huckleberry Finn as well, and I was quite happy being Tom Sawyer.

After the teachers got us under control, they relaxed a bit but they still insisted on being called Sir. Each class had a 'Form Master' and it was to his classroom we all reported each morning. He would then take the roll call by having us all call out a number. The numbers were assigned alphabetically. Anderson was number one, Brown number two, Carter number three, and so on. Starting with Anderson shouting out 'one' he would place a tick against the boy with that number. And I was given the number eighteen and was very relieved. I have never had any trouble at all saying eighteen, in fact, I bet no one can stutter when they say the letter A. Had I got the number twelve I would have been in big trouble. Four would have been difficult as well and, if I got either of them, I probably would have packed it all in and run away to join the circus.

I would sit in silent joy every school day as the Form Master would ask for the count. I would feel like God was indeed on my side as the count went along until seventeen would reverberate through the classroom, and then I'd shout out with the ease of a Shakespearean actor practising in his bathroom 'Eighteen!'

Ah, the simple joys of life. I had become so self-conscious about my stutter that I barely even tried to speak in sentences. If ever I did complete a sentence, it became the source of sheer bliss for the rest of the day. I strutted about the schoolyard like Lenny, spittin' and cussin'!

I began to try and find words that I could substitute for the ones I thought I couldn't say. Big became large, butter became yellow stuff, and Brown just had to be given a nickname, along with anyone called Brian. But I got through it and the beginning of my secondary education was a happy experience. Before I went to 'Tollemache Secondary Modern', I was sure I had been thrown on society's scrap heap, but I soon found out the teachers there had no idea of the concept of a scrap heap; I was extremely happy about that, but I kept it to myself.

I was firmly convinced still that everybody was a wee 'bit bomb happy' and it freed up my decision-making. Before this major breakthrough in my life, I would have gone with the crowd. But now! I decided to support the underdogs of the football world in our area. Tranmere Rovers.

It was a drastic decision indeed. The big football teams on Merseyside were Liverpool and Everton, and those that supported lowly Tranmere Rovers were deemed as being crazy. My newfound logic decided that, if most people were bomb happy, then it didn't matter what they thought. As the years rolled on, I never went back on my decision, and at every Tranmere game I attended at Prenton Park on Borough Road, old Pearhead always came to mind. And so he lived on in my head.

1956 onward
Dad's idiosyncrasies

Pauline

Dad had been used to having a garden to potter in and this little piece of land that came with the house was a challenge to him. The front garden was transformed within weeks. It hadn't had any care for many years, Dad said, and he immediately went to work with horse manure, digging it in and aerating the soil. He then planted a privet hedge and a small rose garden under the front window. As his hedge grew, he trimmed it back into a tidy shape. Every week he went out there with his hedge clippers and meticulously cut any quarter inch of a branch that dared to grow and spoil his tidy shape. As the neighbours began to take an interest in his little patch of land, Dad offered them privet cuttings to grow a hedge of their own. Neighbours on either side took advantage of his generosity and so Dad planted cuttings in their garden and began to grow a hedge like ours. Dad liked things to be tidy so, as their hedge grew, he offered to trim their hedges to match the shape he had in ours.

Over the next few years, 'The Privet Hedge' in Corporation Road got longer and longer as Dad planted cuttings in front gardens whether they wanted them or not. Dad spent any spare time he had going up and down the road trimming the hedges. 'The Hedge' stretched right down the road in front of at least twenty properties. Within a few years of moving into an untidy row of houses, Dad had transformed the entire road with his 'Privet

Hedge.' It now looked a treat as you approached the block of houses with front gardens maintained by the local Irish man.

Dad smoked Embassy cigarettes and they started to put coupons in the packet. When you had saved enough coupons, you could choose to exchange them for gifts from a catalogue. Dad puffed away at his cigarettes saving the coupons for a motorised hedge trimmer.

On the day, his hedge trimmer arrived there was great excitement in the house. Dad immediately went out to trim his hedge in a box shape but with the top in the shape of a wall resembling a fort. High at one side of the gate in a block about two feet square then dropping two feet for another two feet, then rising again into another block, two feet square, and so on. All meticulously measured as he went. Our whole family looked on with pride and pleasure.

As Dad got to the boundary line between our house and the house next door, he didn't stop. Along the neighbour's privet hedge he went, meticulously shaping his fort wall.

"Ye can't do that, Wally; it's not your hedge," Mum reminded him in consternation.

"Ahck! It is my hedge; I gave it to dem, didn't I? Anyway, thaze will luv dis shape."

And he continued to go on his merry way. He was thoroughly enjoying himself. With a grin from ear to ear and singing his Irish songs all the time, the neighbours didn't have the heart to object and spoil his fun. Once he had finished moving to the right he went off to the left. In the space of one weekend, Dad and his motorised hedge trimmer had transformed the entire road. Every week from then on until he died, Dad trimmed the hedges on Corporation Road. He was most definitely a frustrated horticulturist.

The house had also been sadly neglected before we moved in. Dad said there were at least seven sheets of wallpaper on every interior wall and the house would be bigger once it was all removed. We immediately began ripping it all off and redecorating the entire house. It was great fun. From that day on, Mum had a standard phrase, "Don't stand still too long there or ye father will paint ye." He always had his paintbrush in his hand inside, and his much-loved motorised hedge trimmer outside.

Respect for our elders was built into us and they were always called Mr or Mrs. I look back now and fail to understand why our parents used the same titles for each other. Always referring to each other as Mr or Mrs though their peers were the same age as themselves.

Mr McGuiness was our next-door neighbour. He was the same age as my dad and about the same height. Mr McGuiness was a Southern Irish catholic; our dad was Northern Irish Protestant. They were particularly good friends. They called for each other to go for a pint and supported each other home from the *Shamrock Pub*, which was now Dad's local. As they walked home from the pub on Laird Street, we could hear them singing and they would appear around the corner with their arms around each other's shoulders. On arriving at their respective gates; now both painted green by Dad, they would close the gates behind them and continue to sing their Irish songs in their front gardens. Mr McGuiness would harmonise with the high notes as they sang. Head held back and chest puffed up, they would direct their singing toward each other with gestures from their opened arms. This would continue until either Mrs McGuiness or my mother would go out and drag them in.

They also went to the local football matches together and were inseparable … UNTIL the 17th of March, which was St Patrick's Day. Then Dad would shout over the fence to him: "Yer a heathen, that's what ye are, McGuiness, a bloody heathen."

Mr McGuiness would come out of his house rolling up his shirt sleeves. "Ye call me a bloody heathen agin', 'icksie, an' al be puttin' ye on ye arse."

"Yer a bloody heathen, McGuiness, a bloody heathen, come out an' fight like a man instead o' hidin' behind the skirts o' ye Mrs," my father would shout again while he too would start to roll up his sleeves.

At this point 'the wives' would come out of the house and start to drag them both indoors while they would both attempt to protest.

"Let go of me, woman, while a wipes 'im off de face o' de erf."

Somehow at this point in the arguments, the women were stronger than the men and were able to get them both inside.

Mr McGuiness and Dad would then ignore each other all day. If they happened to be in their gardens at the same time, they would shake their fists at each other and growl something that resembled "Geeerrrrawee-witcha."

The following day they would be off to the pub as usual as if it hadn't happened.

The only other day in the year they would fall out would be the 12th of July. It's an Ulster Protestant celebration for Ireland or Orange Lodge Day as Dad would call it. Dad would take his piano accordion outside and prance up and down in front of Mr McGuiness's house playing the orange lodge marches with a huge smile on his face, knowing he was irritating his friend. On hearing the piano accordion, the neighbours would all appear at their front doors or stand in their front gardens knowing what was about to happen and waiting to be entertained. Mr McGuiness would come out and shout at Dad, in the same fashion as he was abused on St Patrick's Day.

"If ye don't git away from me 'ouse, 'icksy, yer'll be feckin sorry, am warnin' ye."

The following day they would be off to the pub as usual.

We knew these two dates must be recognised, being Irish, but never worked out what the aggression between them on these dates was all about. They had a strange relationship.

Johnson, Walter, Pauline & Dad

Dad with Pauline on her wedding day and then sitting in his garden

1959 onward
Corporation Road

Walter

Moving to Corporation Road changed a lot of things for me. It felt as though I had matured into the next phase of my life as I began learning how to spit and cuss. Spitting had many variations, some boys could flick a spit off the end of their tongue, and others could spit green phlegm, but the one I found that suited me best was to spit like I was blowing it out and make a sound like a splat while I was doing it. It took a lot of practice, but soon I had it down pat. I could have been followed around by finding the little blobs that I spat on the pavement every couple of minutes. I wondered why it was that the men, as well as the boys in this neighbourhood, spat and the ones in other neighbourhoods didn't. I concluded that this was a tougher neighbourhood. Men and boys had to show they weren't afraid.

I'd always had a good knowledge of fear. I went through it every night with my imagination and with the ghosts in our bedroom. I knew that fear made my mouth dry up and I would only have fluff where moisture should be. I surmised that as fear made a person's mouth go dry, so spitting, in my ten-year-old mind, was obviously to show you weren't afraid. I imagined that cussing had the same effect. If a man or boy cussed, then he was near to anger, so it was best to be careful around him. Since I was in a very tough environment, I thought it would be best to spit and cuss like the rest of them.

The north end, as it was called, had a lot more men like my dad. They all drank a lot and many loud songs were sung. After the pubs shut at ten-thirty, it was time for the streets to erupt into song. It was common in this area to sing. When my mates and I roamed the streets, we would sing whatever came into our minds. We all heard many songs being sung every night, and when we walked past one of the many pubs we would hear the men singing the night away. It sounded good to me. Life was great. Men knew how to have a good time, and there wasn't a boy amongst us that wasn't looking forward to the day that we could join them in those mysterious places where men congregated, the places they called pubs.

My dad was a major help in my quest for acceptance in this neighbourhood. He was particularly good at fixing bicycles, and as my acquaintances grew, so did the word about my dad. He would always welcome any kid that needed his bike fixed. He would work on the bike with a sense of interest and engage the boys in conversation while he was doing it. I marvelled at his skill, not only with bikes but with the way he would hold their attention. He treated kids differently than other adults did; he made them feel equal, and that was a rare thing. At the time kids were told to hold their tongues and respect their elders, my dad made these kids feel like they were human beings.

When he wasn't fixing bikes, he was building his shed. Dad put together a beautiful big shed that soon took over more than half of our backyard. Then he put shelves in it. Then he put tools in it. It was a sight to behold. I would often go out to the shed when it was pouring rain. I would stand in it listening to the rain pounding like machine guns on the tarmac-covered roof and I would marvel at the fact that not a drop of rain came in.

At the front of the house, we only had about twelve square feet of garden, but in no time at all, we had an array of flowers bursting with colour. I felt proud that our house stood out amongst the other houses – a person walking along the road would suddenly come across a wonderful mishmash of seemingly disorganized, but nonetheless, highly effective, flower attack on their senses.

My history lessons had a powerful effect on my thoughts about Dad. He was already teetering on the brink of my disrespect because of his drinking and the fighting with my mother. I had now begun to doubt him for fighting for a country that allowed its kids to run around in rags while some kids wore silk pyjamas, but I had to admit that while I had lost some respect for him over his choice to fight for such a country, plus the fighting with my mother, his drive and energy in the way he fixed up the house, painting everything that couldn't take a roll of wallpaper, building a shed, planting a glorious flower garden and most of all the way he had of charming the local kids were winning me back to him. Once again, he seemed worthy of my admiration, and I began to feel a renewed pride in him.

Mum liked the new neighbourhood because she was now closer to her sisters who lived only a few streets away from us. I was glad that she lived closer to her sisters because now we would never have to go through another midnight walk in the park which had left a scar on Pauline's psyche for life.

Inheriting Mums Spirituality
1960s

Pauline

The first time I experienced any spiritual strangeness I can remember was when Uncle Frank died. He had been in hospital for what seemed a long time and I cannot remember what it was exactly that he died of. Mum told me I had to visit Uncle Frank with her. I was twelve years old at the time and remember Mum taking me with her on the bus. As I walked into the hospital ward I felt as though I had bumped into a huge inflatable rubber balloon. It took my breath away and I gasped as I entered the ward.

"What's the problem with ye, Pauline?" asked Mum.

"I felt as though I bumped into a big balloon," I said, which was the only way I could explain it.

Uncle Frank lay still in the bed and as we approached him, I could see that his bed had more light around it than the others did. We sat quietly at the side of the bed until he opened his eyes.

"She's here, Frank," Mum said, and I looked at her in astonishment. I didn't know Uncle Frank had asked to see me especially.

Uncle Frank held out his hand to me and smiled weakly. I gently held his hand and a strong surge ran through me. I felt as though my spirit had completely engulfed him. Uncle Frank acknowledged it by giving me a small nod of the head, then he sighed and closed his eyes again, and I felt his hand go limp in mine.

"Come on now, Pauline, and let Uncle Frank get some rest," Mum said a few minutes later.

I left the hospital with a strange feeling, 'knowing' that something had transpired between us.

Uncle Frank died that night. His was an Irish wake and we gathered in his home with my aunt and all the relatives, while Uncle Frank was placed in his open coffin in the front parlour. The day before his funeral, people came and paid their last respects to him while he lay in his coffin. We supplied everybody with tea and biscuits right through until the evening when the men had finished work and gathered in the house and the alcohol began to be consumed. People walked around the house singing and talking to Uncle Frank as though he was still alive.

"Here's ye favourite, Frank, are ye ready boys!! Altogether!

Oh, Patrick McGinty an Irish man of note,

Came into a fortune and bought 'imself a goat."

Anything they wanted to say to Uncle Frank in private was said behind the closed door of the parlour. When they had finished their private conversation with him, the door was opened again and everybody was allowed to wander in and out.

An Irish wake goes on throughout the night and nobody goes to bed. As a twelve-year-old, I found it hard to stay awake and, in the early hours of the morning, I wandered into the hall and sat on the bottom stair with my elbows on my knees and my chin in my hands. As I stared ahead of me, Uncle Frank came out of the front parlour. I wasn't afraid or shocked, I remember just smiling at him.

He came and sat beside me and asked how I was feeling. "I'm fine," I said. "How are you feeling, Uncle Frank?"

"Could not be happier, lass; could not be happier. No more pain." He smiled "Ave always loved yer Aunty Lil an' a knows she will be upset fer a while. But a want ye t'tell 'er that al be lookin' after 'er still. Me brother will be waitin' fer them in Ireland an' a wants them t'go an' visit 'im fer a while. It will do them a power o'good. T'ings will be well taken care of while they're away, an' ave left them well provided fer. Me brother will explain. Will ye tell dem dat?"

"A will, Uncle Frank," I said. He stood up and gave me a big smile and walked back into the parlour.

Just then Mum walked into the hall.

"What are ye doin' sittin' there, luv?" she asked.

"Ave just been talkin' to Uncle Frank," I replied.

"Oh 'av ye!" she remarked "An' what did 'ee ave t'say?"

I repeated our conversation word for word. She wasn't shocked and said she would tell Aunty Lil. Because it was the middle of the night, my childhood reasoning kept me thinking I may have dreamt it all. When Aunty Lil felt stronger, she went to Ireland to visit Uncle Franks' brother. The family farm had been sold and Aunty Lil was presented with half the proceeds. When Mum repeated this fact before our family, she just looked at me and with a wink gave me a half smile, so I just smiled back.

A few years later, my Uncle Freddie was ill in hospital. Again, Mum said I was to visit him. I was around fourteen years old. This strange feeling of bumping into a rubber balloon was with me again as I entered the ward. His bed was also surrounded by light. Uncle Freddie opened his eyes and smiled at me. He didn't say anything and Mum told me to kiss him. As I did, the same feeling of energy that I felt with Uncle Frank ran between our bodies. With this energy came a strong feeling of empathy for him. I found it hard not to let him see me crying and I wanted to hug him but was afraid of hurting him. That night Uncle Freddie died. During that night, I had a vivid dream. I was talking to Uncle Freddie and he gave me a message for my aunt. In telling Mum I realised that this was something more than a dream. But Mum never explained it properly to me; she simply passed on the messages I had been given.

This strange 'gift' I was becoming aware of then started to frighten me. As there was always talk about 'the next world,' 'the spirit world' and a loose acceptance of a God around our house, I had heard about 'The Angel of Death.' Though I didn't ask Mum what this Angel did, I was convinced that this was what I was. If I visited anyone that was ill, they would die. I couldn't talk to anyone about it, as I didn't want to frighten people away from me. I made a definite promise to myself that I would avoid anyone that was ill for fear I made them die. Anytime Mum asked me to visit a sick friend or relative in hospital, I began to invent all sorts of reasons why I couldn't go. If Mum tried to insist, I would throw a tantrum and raise my Irish paddy until she gave up. There was no way I was going to be responsible for anyone else dying.

It was commonly known that Mum had a strong intuitive/spiritual ability, speaking to the recently dead on many occasions. Mum's eyes would flicker from yours to the guide that stands behind you at challenging times throughout your life and she claimed they were speaking to her. Throughout my childhood, I watched her do this as she read the tea leaves in cups for neighbours, friends, and family members. She would also read tarot cards. When I asked her how she did that, her answer was,

"Interpreting the shapes of the tea leaves keeps me focused on a small, enclosed space, and as I do I check in to the person's guide and their aura. With the cards, it is a visual for both me and the person I am reading. I can tap into their being and, as we both look at the face of the card with its meaning, the right words about their concerns and events that are about to happen pop into my head. But it is a responsibility and must never be abused as some people aren't ready to hear that a loved one is about to die, or a tragic event is about to happen. You therefore must be selective in what you pass on. I'll teach you how to do this when you're older because you have the gift."

Mum also had what her family called 'the evil eye' which,

translated, meant she could see and feel an evil spirit. She could walk into a room full of strangers and be immediately drawn to a black aura. Standing stock still, she would bore her eyes into the back of their skull, so much that they could feel it and would turn to make eye contact with her. She would scowl until the person couldn't take this powerful gaze anymore and would usually leave the room if they could. If they didn't, Mum would turn and leave the room, saying words such as "I can't be in the same room or breathe the same air as evil; I feel sick."

She would talk of speaking to the spirit of someone deceased, and that person had given her some message or was sending support to their loved ones through her. She could also sense when her kids were trying to lie about something, and she would stare at us and take on a scowl that was saying, "Don't try lying to me; I can see your soul."

I was very close to my siblings and another time something strange happened to me was when Walter was on holiday in Spain. I'd been helping Mum with the washing in the kitchen and my nervous debility (as Mum called it) began to vibrate in me. Mum would keep an eye on me at these times and help me to settle down. "Everybody's out," she said, "Make the most of it and go and sit in the front room and do that meditating yer've just learned."

Sitting in the front parlour staring at a blank wall would calm my nerves and I would then close my eyes and meditate.

John Lennon had brought the Maharishi to a concert in the Empire Theatre in Liverpool and asked us all to line up to learn how to meditate, I was almost first in the queue.

Emptying my mind as the Maharishi had taught me, I learned to stare at blank spaces to settle me before meditation, and so I was staring at the blank wall above the piano when I saw Walter's face. He was behind bars and he was shouting for me. He was saying "Get me out, Pauline; get me out!!" Just at that point, Mum walked into the room and it shocked me back to the here and now.

I looked at her with a wide-eyed expression on my face.

"What's troublin' ye, Pauline?" Mum asked.

"Ave just seen our Walter, Mum. He was behind bars and was crying for me t'get 'im out," I replied.

She had a troubled expression on her face and stared at me for a while, then said, "A new 'eed get 'imself inter trouble over there!" And went back to the kitchen and her work.

And my vision was right as he was deported back to England the following day.

Being an Angel of Death was something I didn't want to be, but having this strange psychic gift was okay by me. I could live with that.

1959 onward
Researching the Wars

Walter

Mr Siltreen was our history teacher. He didn't give out books. He just stood out in front of the class leaning his bum on the front of his desk and spoke like he was telling us a story. He was popular because he didn't mind if anyone fell asleep during his class. He only insisted on silence and any snorers were woken up to the sound of the cane whacking only a few inches away from his nose.

He told us about the past from his perspective. He had clearly read all the books and digested them and now we were to be the ones that would benefit from his years of all that reading. There was no political concept to his teaching, no bias, no national pride, and there was to be no nurturing of any more cannon fodder for the likes of General 'Butcher' Haig in his classroom. He derided the British officers in World War One 'Chinless Wonders', he called them. He said that the younger officers led from the front and went over the top of the trenches first, where they were the first to be shot, thus leaving the men without an officer when they needed one most, while the most senior officers stayed well back and still thought in terms of a cavalry charge, a thought that routinely ordered thousands of men into a hail of machine gun bullets.

His history lessons didn't come in any particular order. He might start talking about the stone age men but would finish off talking about the First or Second World War. He aroused my interest in history when, at the end of his first class, a class on Hannibal crossing the Alps, which somehow weaved into a detailed account of Edmund Hilary climbing Mount Everest, which then went on to a story of some people in Switzerland that ate arsenic from an early age to make them live longer, and then went back to Hannibal.

"In all the battles that Hannibal had, he only lost eight hundred men! Why was that?" but he wouldn't wait for an answer!

"It is because most soldiers in a battle have trouble killing someone if they can see the enemy's eyes. However, when they turned their backs that was another story. Soldiers most often got killed while running away. Hannibal's army never ran away, so his soldiers never turned their backs on the enemy and that is why he only lost eight hundred men."

He would stop talking now and then to take a sip of something that he had hidden in his desk. Then, after smacking his lips and emitting a small but very satisfied sigh, he would look up at the ceiling for a few seconds to regain his train of thought.

"Furthermore," he went on, "before World War Two, it had always been assumed that a soldier would kill a man simply because his country and its leaders told him to. They thought that the instinct of self-preservation would force any man to kill another man that was trying to kill him. It was simple logic. Put a man in a position where it's his life or Joe Bloggs, poor old Joe Bloggs was sure to lose. Right?"

Then, in one of those amazing coincidences that have followed me throughout my life, he came out of his usual dream state and looked me right in the eyes. Then answered my question without me asking it.

"However," he said, "during World War Two, a United States Army brigadier, a man named S.L.A Marshall, who was to become the official historian for World War Two by the way, this officer by means of interviewing men just after they had been in combat found that out of any hundred men on any given firing line, in any battle, an average of only fifteen to twenty percent would take any part with their weapons."

He looked around the class as if he were curious as to what our reaction would be.

"Most of the men couldn't kill another human being, not even to save their lives," he said.

I could hardly believe it. My teacher had just confirmed what my dad had said. Most people couldn't kill each other! Not even in war.

Mr Siltreen smiled a sad smile.

"You are lucky, boys, to know such a thing beforehand. Most boys think that killing in a battle comes easy. You only see the glory that the soldiers have when they come home. But I see something different in you lot. Am I right?"

Nobody answered.

"What about you, Mr Potman? Could you stick a cold bayonet into a wounded man's gut?"

Percy Potman, who had been moved to the B stream with me, looked like he was horrified.

"Let me tell you about the bayonet. If two opposing groups of soldiers are charging each other with bayonets, an exceptionally large proportion of both sides will invariably remember an urgent appointment elsewhere. Do you get my drift, boys?"

Nobody answered.

"It's because they can see each other's faces. They can see each other's eyes, and in those eyes, they can see their own self."

He paused for effect and then smiled right at me.

"So, why is the very idea of sticking a sharpened piece of cold steel into a man made to be a much harder task than it would be if you turned your back?"

"Their eyes," I said.

"Precisely. And why is that?"

"Because we can see ourselves in their eyes," I said.

"Exactly. And if we turn our backs to them then what don't they see?"

"Our eyes," I heard myself say.

Mr Siltreen smiled like he had found a young prodigy.

"What is your name, boy?"

"Hicks," I said.

"Well, Mr Hicks, will you please tell me and the whole class, in your own words, what would probably happen to you if you turned your back on a group of men that were running at you with bayonets on the end of their rifles."

As usual, when I was completely engrossed in something, I forgot that I stuttered.

"They would probably stick the bayonet in my back," I said.

"So, what does that tell us?" he said.

I was baffled. I just stared into his eyes until he looked for an answer somewhere else, but he soon gave up.

"It tells us about the law of self-preservation. We all have it. It's the one thing that nobody can deny having. If we can see our enemy, then it is hard to kill our enemy because deep down inside us we know that he is just like we are, and that part of us, that part of us that is connected to the whole human race, won't let us kill a being that is just like us."

He paused, then looked around the classroom, his gaze went from one boy to another.

"Is there anyone here that feels that they could live without feeling bad about themselves if they knew that they had killed a man after they had looked him in the eyes, and then to realise that they had killed this man merely because they had been told to by a chinless wonder? If they'd killed two men, would they feel even worse? Does one death only have half as much effect as two deaths would have? What about if you ordered thousands to be killed?

But you hadn't seen their eyes? Would you still feel bad? Probably not. However, would those unseen eyes come to haunt you in your dreams? Would you feel like you had to justify your orders to drive away those thousands of questioning eyes that come to haunt you in the wee hours? I think so. I think you would have to try to find something noble in the killing you ordered, either that or face up to the demons of the night."

He took a deep breath and looked like he'd seen his fate and had resigned himself to it.

"History is history. It's gone. You can take it or leave it. You can sleep through my class like the dead men that have gone by, make all the same mistakes that they did, and you can call your mistakes tradition. We all die in the end anyway, and tradition isn't such a bad thing, it helps us along while we are alive. But always remember this. History reflects your own kind, history tells you who and what you are, and if you take nothing else from my class you can at least take this from me: History is written by the winners."

The bell rang.

"Class dismissed," he said.

He leaned his bum on his desk with his arms crossed and watched as we streamed out and formed two lines in the hallway. I tried to imagine what it would be like to be him. One class stream out and then another class streamed in. Then, no doubt he would take a sip of whatever gave him strength and start talking again to the next group of disinterested boys. He caught me looking at him, and he must have read my mind because he looked right at me, shrugged his shoulders, and smiled a half-smile. Then he turned away and walked to the window to gaze out at a world that in my mind he obviously saw as being completely 'bomb happy'!

Bidston Hill Windmill Birkenhead

1960s
High School, starting work, and Rock and Roll

Pauline

During the first year of my life on Corporation Road, I took the bus to the junior school I attended, Christ Church School on Borough Road. The schooling system at that time was a junior school from age five to eleven/twelve. The eleven-plus examination was then sat by everyone and, if you passed you would go on to a high school in the area, if you failed you went to a secondary modern school. I sat the eleven-plus examination and passed to go to Park High School for Girls.

My parents were so proud of me. Mum and Dad went about telling everyone: "Our Pauline is going to High School."

I was the talk of the neighbourhood for a while. Mum contacted the school I was about to attend to ask if they had a second-hand school uniform department. She couldn't afford to buy me new school clothes and the amount of sports equipment that was needed for me was a problem Mum needed to work on.

The second-hand uniform room in the school I was about to attend had old sports equipment also and Mum was excited for me. "We can get everything you need here, Pauline. Isn't that just grand."

Mum picked out a school uniform that had belonged to a sixteen-year-old who had just left school. "This'll do yer fine,"

Mum said as she held up this huge maroon pinafore dress. "I'll take it in and put a hem on it and if ye look after it it'll last ye till ye finish school," she said, smiling. We picked out a lacrosse stick, a tennis racket, a hockey stick, a school satchel, and two pairs of shoes, one for wearing every day and one for sports. Then a maroon mackintosh, and a grey blazer, a beret for my head in winter and a boater hat for summer. I was as thrilled as Mum. We carried them home and set about putting tucks in this and hems on that. Dad sanded, stained, and polished the sports equipment and Mum made me a cotton drawstring bag to put them all in.

As I stood before Mum and Dad wearing all my 'new' clothes, they looked at me with pride. Mum escorted me to the bus and waved me off to my first morning at this school saying: "Yer'll make many new friends, it'll be lots of fun, and remember to be respectful to the teachers!"

I walked into the hall for my first day at this school and felt everybody whispering and laughing at me in groups. I had arrived looking like a pack horse in comparison. Their clothes all fitted them 'now', and I saw no sign of any one of them with second-hand anything. The twelve-inch hems on my pinafore and mackintosh were rather obvious and seemed to cause titters of laughter as I dragged my drawstring floral cotton bag across the hall. The other girls all had neat leather cases for their sports equipment. My shoes were a size too big for me, but Mum had bought them knowing I would grow into them so they were packed with newspaper in the toes. My heel would hit the floor a split second before the splat of the sole arrived. I must have looked like the school clown. I also seemed to be the smallest and skinniest person there. I did as Dad had told me and walked up to various groups of girls to meet them, but they all turned away from me, laughing.

Lunchtime arrived and we lined up outside the dining hall to pay for our week's lunches. The cost was six pence per day, being two and sixpence for the whole week, which was a half crown. My family received welfare support for school dinners and so I handed over my welfare dinner token. The teacher looked up at me and asked, "What is this, dear?"

My face began to burn. "It's my dinner token, miss."

"Just one moment I need to ask another teacher about these," she said and left her chair. All the girls were giggling and whispering behind their hands again and I was engulfed with humiliation. I wanted to grab my things and leave this school there and then.

My time at this school was not a happy one. Dad encouraged me to "show 'em what yer made of … yer as good as any one of 'em and better than most."

We had only recently moved into this area and when I was seen in my school uniform the girls in this area decided I must have thought I was better than them and wouldn't befriend me. The girls in the high school I was attending looked down on me because I came from a poor area and I didn't have the clothes and equipment they had. Consequently, I concentrated on my school and homework because I had no distractions. I studied hard so that I wouldn't let my parents down and received high marks when I eventually sat my school 'O' levels at the age of sixteen, but leaving this school to start work was the best day of my life. I had been out of my 'class.'

Miss Rice was my maths teacher and after asking me if I was considering going to university, I told her, "No. Mum wants me to start work to help with the housekeeping, Miss Rice." She handed me a letter at the end of the day asking me to give this to my mum and dad.

Mum read it and exclaimed, "What a lovely letter, Pauline. It could be used as a reference for a job. She says you should think of going on to university as you're clever enough. If ye would rather do that, luv, I'll see if I can make it happen?"

"No, Mum. I've had enough of school. I want to start working now."

My auburn hair and green eyes made me an attractive teenager and I loved to dance. It was the 1960s, and I was lucky enough to live around Merseyside when the world had Beatle mania. Every Friday and Saturday night my friend and I would get the ferry across the Mersey to Liverpool. We could then be found in any one of Liverpool's many clubs, rock and rolling through every dance. If a 'fella' didn't ask us up to dance, my friend and I would dance together until two of them came to 'split us up.'

Winkle picker shoes with 6" stiletto heels were something I quickly adapted to and jammed my feet into them every day, tottering around, appreciating the extra height these shoes gave my small slight frame.

Having naturally curly hair was too 'square' in these times and I put large fat foam rubber rollers in it every night, trying to straighten it to produce the sleek bouffant style that Dusty Springfield made popular in our time. Unfortunately, one puff of wind or downpour of rain would make it frizz up again and so I used hair lacquer. This was part of my essential wardrobe and was as necessary to me as lipstick. I sprayed my hair until it was as stiff as a board and looked set in concrete before I went through the door of the house, then proceeded to spray every wisp of hair that escaped the bouffant shape on which I had so painstakingly worked.

Skin-tight miniskirts and clothes, and stiff, starched, net petticoats that held out a felt skirt under a waspy belt were two of the main fashion choices. The petticoats were my favourite because they didn't prevent me from rock and rolling and they swirled out beautifully when I twirled around. In my mind, this made a lovely picture, but on reflection, I can see that my pink net petticoats, skinny legs, and six-inch stiletto heels, must have had me resembling a pink flamingo in a frenzy when I was dancing. At the time though, I felt like 'the bees' knees' and stepped out every weekend in full war paint resembling a fairy on a Christmas Tree.

The boys we fancied wore what we called, Teddy Boy clothes – suits with long single-breasted jackets that had sleeves that ended halfway down their hands. The collars of these jackets were velvet. The pants were 'drainpipes 'and their shoes were winkle pickers, e.g. pointed toes. They used Brylcream on their long straight hair to slick it to the back of their head where it met in the middle. This was called a D.A. which meant a duck's arse. The front was pulled forward over their eyes. We used to call this style a Tony Curtis or an Elvis hairdo.

The *Mardi Gras Club* on the left at the top of Matthew Street in Liverpool was a jazz club and our favourite venue. *The Cavern* was too small for our liking but sometimes we would finish at the *Mardi Gras* at about 10 pm and walk down the hill to sit on the top step of *The Cavern* club listening to whichever band was on at the time. *The Cavern Club* was a basement of a large Victorian building and to enter it you descended the stairs from the street level. We visited in the early days to listen to the Beatles but the cigarette smoke was thick and you could not see your hand in front of you so we would sit outside just listening. John Lennon came out one time to have a cigarette and we chatted. My friend Irene told him it was my birthday soon and he said the next song was for me. We heard him announce this when he went back in, and some years later when the Beatles were famous, Irene and I rummaged through our brains trying to remember which song he sang for me. We couldn't remember it.

Life was exciting and fun. Boyfriends were never a shortage to me and I would have dates throughout the week with the latest 'feller' that I had met on Saturday night. Heartaches were plenty as most teenagers of any generation experience, but the plus we had was the newfound freedom our generation had with its 'flower power' and Hippies, 'Hari Krishna's' and 'love not war' values, pushed upon the unsuspecting world.

Drinking alcohol was something I wasn't good at; 'one Babycham and I'm anybody's, was my favourite expression. I didn't smoke, never took drugs, and didn't tell anyone that I still went to church on Sunday.

The peer pressure was more than I wanted to cope with and I knew I would have my leg pulled if they found out that I was a Sunday school teacher, so I began to lead a double life. I attended Bidston Parish Church – St Oswald's – because it was like having a singsong every Sunday morning. The Reverend Singleton had been an army chaplain and he would play the guitar and beef up the rhythm of the hymns. I'm sure he must have been the first to do this in his time. He would give me a bible story every Sunday and ask me to read it throughout the week and teach that to the kids at my next Sunday class. I would read it a couple of times through the week and then deliver it without notes the next Sunday. On this day he stood at the door of the room I was in, listening to my interaction with the children. I started okay and was teaching them about Lott and his wife leaving Sodom, and then I began to improvise.

"And Lott said t' God … ar eh God, look what yerve gone and dun! Yerve turned me wife inta a pile of salt! Oo's gunna cook me tea now?" And I looked up to see his head lowering into his wide-open hand and fingers covering his face as he shook his head. I guess I should have stuck to the correct script but I would guarantee those kids would remember my version more than the bible story!

My younger brothers had long grown out of wanting to listen to the stories I used to read to them and being a Sunday school teacher allowed me to read to children and watch their faces. They would listen in awe to the magical happenings that I would read to them from the bible with my modern-day twist to them. I had inherited my father's ability to tell a story, set the scene, and involve my listeners in all I told them. Looking back, I can see some of the distorted messages I was giving these young impressionable minds. I had an audience and often made the stories up as I went along, just like my father did. There were times when I had finished the story but it didn't resemble the bible at all.

When we were children, God was mentioned around our house as an invisible member of the family, along with the spirit world, fairies, and leprechauns. If any personal possession had been moved overnight, the leprechauns had been up to their mischief again. The fairies were kind; they used to leave sweets under your pillow if you were unhappy or leave a penny in exchange for a tooth that had come out. They paid for these because they needed them for gravestones. If we asked for anything extravagant or posed a question that Mum decided we should give some thought to, she would say:

"'ave a word with God t'night an' see what 'ee says." By the following morning, of course, we had forgotten what it was we needed answers to.

Dancing and singing in my teenage years gave me the outlet I needed to express my 'love of life.' I was exuberant, bubbly, and had an infectious sense of humour; gathering people because I surrounded myself with amusement.

When I left school, I went to work in the office of an engineering company. I was so proud that I could earn money to help Mum with the household expenses. My sister Babs was already working and helping Mum so she led the way for us all to follow.

During those times when everyone knew everyone in our community. The milkman, Ted, who called early each morning to deliver our milk, was thrilled when I found a job nearby. He saw me through the front window.

"Pauline, luv," he shouted, indicating for me to go outside as he had something to tell me. I stepped out.

"I finish my round at St James Church at 8 o'clock each mornin'. I'm then goin' back to the depot in Old Bidston Road with an empty cart, so I can give ye a lift to work as I'm passin' your door each day and the engineering company yer'll be working at is right next door to my depot." He grinned from ear to ear as he said this because he was able to help me.

"Oh, thanks so much, Ted. That would be really helpful," I answered, and so each morning I stood at our gate waiting for Ted. The electric milk carts almost silently purred along the roads. It had a compact domed cab big enough for the driver only and the small truck had a roof over a deck that held the milk crates. Ted would pull up in front of me each morning, jump out of his driver's cab and move the crates to one side so I had room to sit with my legs dangling over the back of the deck. Mum gave me a piece of a plastic tablecloth to place on the deck for me to sit on so my clothes wouldn't get spoiled. Off I went every morning, my bag on my lap and the electric truck quietly purring along the road on my way to work. If it was raining, I sat there with my umbrella open over me no doubt looking a little like Mary Poppins.

The neighbours became used to seeing me.

"Mornin', Pauline. Lovely day eh!"

"Mornin', Mrs Foster," I would call back. "Mum said she'll call and see ye near midday."

"Thanks, luv. 'ave a lovely day."

"Allo, Pauline luv."

"Allo, Mr Wentworth."

I'd be shouting to each and every person I passed by. They might only wave and I would wave back like the queen as I sailed along seated on my floating throne. People talked of telling the time by me when they saw me pass on my trip to work! It was a great start to my day. I always arrived at work with a smile on my face.

The milk cart - my transport to work.

Mum was able to buy a few luxuries for the house now Babs and I were working and we hired a bigger television from Radio Rental. My family had gone up in the world and was now being classed as one of the posh ones in the street because we had a piano **and** a television. If something special was being televised, the neighbours would sit around our living room watching the TV while the kids sat on the floor.

My interest in my singers began with Flanagan and Allan, Bing Crosby, Gracie Fields, Vera Lyn, and The Andrew Sisters on the television and I could sing every one of their songs. As a teenager of course my singers changed to Cliff Richard, The Beatles, Elvis, Tom Jones, Dusty Springfield, and all the 60's songs and music that filled our house constantly. Most Saturday nights Dad would bring those in the pub back to our house as he played the piano and we would have a singsong singing some of the war songs.

Mum would often comment that having Dad and me in the house at the same time was like living in the middle of a tornado. I had an amazing amount of energy that fueled my being. Why walk when you can run? And why stop because the dark has set in?

I had more energy than almost any other person I knew. (Apart from Dad.) If I was determined to complete something, anything, no matter what, the time of day or night wasn't an issue. I never ran out of energy and sometimes I would feel that having to sleep was a waste of my time. At times, this energy coursed through my body for no particular reason. My nerves would be vibrating and, as I aged, I started jogging in the mornings, which helped, or I would sometimes get out in the fresh air and walk the dog until my nervousness settled. For me, being alive was action! I was not a person to be found lying on the couch or in my bed if I wasn't ill. My only health problem was I began suffering from migraines as a teenager and then I had to take to my bed sometimes for one or two days. They would make me nauseous and a really bad one could make me blind. Migraines were the only blight on my health through to my mid-fifties.

My childhood before marriage was typically Irish. Six of us in the house, plus the dog, family friends, and neighbours calling day and night was the life I was used to. Constant chatter, laughter, Dad playing the piano, singing, and even bickering and fighting with my brothers and sister, but that crazy, funny, out-there love of living, didn't prepare me for my painful lonely marriage that lay ahead.

My daughter was born in the first year of my marriage and my son three years later. I discovered that my husband was an alcoholic and a gambler, and my life was spent working full-time to supply my family's needs.

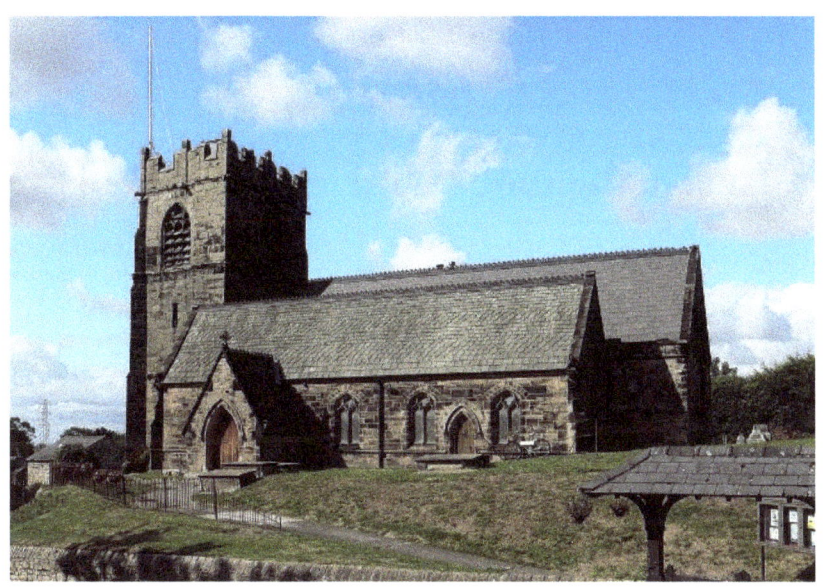

St Oswald's Church Bidston Birkenhead where Pauline was a Sunday school teacher.

From the 1960s until leaving school

Walter

I was one of a gang of 'tough' lads in our neighborhood. This was the façade that we all showed daily. Sissies don't live in our neck of the woods! We might be critical of a member of our gang and sometimes wrestle and get them in headlocks, but it was always a show. This was us learning our defense mechanisms, never with malice. If an interloper stumbled onto our patch and tried to pick a fight with one of us, every kid in the vicinity would race to his defence. "He is one of us! You take him on, and you take us all on!"

When I entered the sacred halls of Tolly and found Mr Siltreen waiting there I knew this was the best thing that had happened to me so far in my life. Mr Siltreen was one of two drugs that pulled me into school every day; history was the second. My parents made sure we had books to help our education and we owned the sacred Encyclopedia Britannica (we had to wash our hands before we could touch them) plus atlases and history books which lay around for us all to use. The school had a library for my research and yet my brain was always eager to find answers to my many questions and this became a daily obsession. During my four years at Tolly, if history wasn't on my daily curriculum, Mr Siltreen would chat with me when school finished for the day. He never once told me he didn't have time or had only a minimal amount of time. I would hover outside his last history class and as the class was dismissed, he would open the door to let that class out and look at me with a half-smile on his face and with a nod would say, "Come in, Mr Hicks. How can I help you today?" I had so many questions and needed to know the answers – now! He would answer my questions in his usual way – by turning them into a story. I also developed this way of imparting information over the years. Telling a story had hooks and lines of thread that knitted together a picture that would settle into my memory, never to be forgotten.

My brother Johnson followed me into Tolly, and his introduction was easier because me and my mate Allan walked him in – we threw him in the bushes for his flight into his new life, but we also let everyone know, this kid is my brother, mess with him and you have me an' Allan to deal with. I do feel it helped Johnson to settle into the school and I was confident that enough had been done to stop the bullies right from the start and continue for his five years in the school.

My final day at Tolly was a sad day for me. I do believe it was for Mr Siltreen as well. He had spoken to me about my interest in history and encouraged me not to let it fade away. We never spoke of university as Tolly School catered to working-class kids and didn't churn out university students. Every mum looked forward to their son starting work and bringing home money. That's how it was in the North End of Birkenhead.

I knew that researching history would be something I would continue for the rest of my life and so didn't feel the need to attend a university.

Dad took me to Cammell Lairds and organized an apprenticeship for me as a welder. I'd like to say I was grateful for the opportunity, but it was wasted on me. Walking through that gate every day carved a cavernous hole in the pit of my stomach. I was out of my 'comfort zone.' This job was not for me. I needed to be doing something that ignited my curiosity, for me to then spend time digesting it – sitting spaced out in my private inner world and then putting it all into action, breaking my thirst for new knowledge down into information that can be absorbed and used to develop my character to form solid opinions on life. And then to make a difference in this world. But learning how to weld?! No! That didn't fit into the person I was becoming. Knowing how to weld would not save the world!

I tried hard for over a year until I had to announce to Mum and Dad my feelings about the job. The rows in the house were at full bore from both my mum and my dad, BUT! I just couldn't walk through the gates of Cammell Lairds for one more day! It was killing my soul! I walked away from welding and from home.

Mr Siltreens influence over me etched into my soul the need for Peace, not War, Love not War. We were raised in the aftermath of World War Two where more than eighty-five million people perished, infrastructure was destroyed, and for what? We heard horrific stories from the returned soldiers and the women left at home to bury the dead, navigate bombs, and the destruction of their homes. In our family, we lost our oldest sister Sarah during the war. Dad was drowning his memories in beer every night, meaning Mum and us kids lived in fear of him coming home. Both the streets we Hicks' kids had lived on to date highlighted the devastation of people and infrastructure that the war caused. Amputees were the norm. As I researched the wars, I felt passionate about how I can be involved in actions to stop war from ever happening again. There must have been thousands of 'Mr Siltreens' in schools across the globe teaching that war must stop now. We were in unison in the Western world decrying social archetypes and roles, pre-established patterns of behaviours as well as ego-based social and economic structures.

Millions of people across the world began to withdraw identification with a collective conceptual identity because the insanity of the collective was so obvious. Mr Siltreen encouraged us to stop believing and participating in society's collective fantasies and false narratives. Don't be sheep, don't follow blindly, think for yourselves, and challenge the narrative of the authorities. Demonstrate love and non-violence.

I walked out of my job at Cammell Lairds with a determined mind that I was going to make a difference. I wasn't arrogant enough to think I would do this all on my own, but I needed to be part of a larger movement to help make the changes necessary that would move toward a peaceful world.

I let my hair grow long and tied it back in a bun. Colourful shirts and loose pants replaced jeans and neat shirts. And shoes were not a part of my latest look. I became a Hippie and formed a local group. I purchased leather from the tannery near Woodside in Birkenhead and made belts, bags, headbands necklets, and bracelets. I also cut leather soles to replace shoes and slit openings in them to weave strips of leather or twisted hessian through to hold them in place and plait these strips around the lower leg. This was how I created an income. We would wander the streets singing and talking of 'peace not war.' Handing out flowers and spreading the word of Flower Power. (Flower Power was a slogan used during the late sixties and early seventies as a symbol of passive resistance.) The Vietnam War was now raging, and we sat with our placards in peaceful protest outside government buildings and places where government officials were gathered. A group of us rented a flat together near the Claughton Arms in Birkenhead. We sat around discussing peace, making love, and smoking dope! On one occasion, we sat singing in a demonstration against the Vietnam War throughout the night on the roundabout called Charing Cross in Birkenhead. The police that were sent to move us on actually sat around the edge of our group singing with us until dawn broke.

Earning money wasn't a priority in my life: I was living my truth.

A group of us decided to travel to Spain and spread the Hippie movement by demonstrating that it doesn't have a language barrier. We sat smoking dope on the beaches gathering those interested until we were a large gathering, but a couple of us were recognized as the leaders. We were arrested, imprisoned, and then deported back to England. We had made our mark in Spain, and I knew that the group we had gathered there would now continue without me.

Arriving home after being jailed and thrown out of Spain was something newsworthy in the 1960/70s and the Birkenhead Newspaper decided to 'shame' us by covering our arrest and deportation. They explained what these Hippie people were up to. But we silently thanked them for promoting our cause and felt it had been a successful trip. We made it into the local papers and became aware that news of any description was good for the cause. Our numbers swelled. My parents were ready to disown me!

We began to research spirituality. We bought crystals and studied their healing powers. We would spend some nights in the woods to blend in and be at one with Nature. These sojourns healed my soul, and I realized I needed to find my own space in Nature periodically throughout my life to enable me to live with myself.

London was a favourite place to have silent protests outside the Palace of Westminster where Parliament sat, and Number 10 Downing Street when they were having dignitaries from war-torn countries.

Along with my brother Johnson and a few of my Hippie friends, we moved to Newquay in Cornwall for about twelve months. We slept on the beaches until we found a cave. There were seven of us and when the tide came in, we were marooned in our cave so had to be aware of this when we planned our daily activities. We needed money for food so Johnson and I both worked in a hotel. This worked out well as we could get a warm shower there, and for me pulling pints behind the bar was perfect. Our wages fed us all. During the time I was in Newquay, I taunted death and am lucky to be here now to tell my story. On one occasion I fell asleep on a surfboard and was drifting out to sea. Luckily, I was spotted and brought back to shore. This period of time, when I look back, was one of the best times of my life. Johnson and I shared many happenings that young men of all generations will sometimes be faced with, and how we dealt with them will be secrets we'll take to our graves.

And then I met my American Hippie girlfriend who was visiting Newquay. She came back to Birkenhead with me, but her family was screaming and demanding she must go home. And so, with love in my heart, I decided to go back with her to Oregon on the west coast of America. Within months we were married and the following year my son Matthew Walter was born.

The Hippie movement stood for a loosening of the rigid egoic structures in the psyche of humanity. Peace, not War, and Love, not War had been our call to the world, and being determined about changing the war lords' psyche as we sat in peaceful protest all over the Western world. But taking drugs was our downfall until it became not 'cool' to be seen as a Hippie. The movement itself ended but it did leave a void seen as an opening and not just within those who were part of the movement. It was now possible for ancient Eastern wisdom and spirituality to move west and play an essential part in the awakening of global consciousness. I was happy that the years I had silently protested and demonstrated peace, not war produced this result and made those years have value.

To date had been a good life for me. I was aware that some Hippies were in the movement for drugs alone and no responsibility, but I was always truthful to the cause. I wasn't one of the periphery drug takers only. I took the title of Hippie seriously. Yes, I did the drugs and practised free love but that was my private life. My purpose in being a Hippie was to make a change in the psyche of the warlords of this world. This drove me daily by reading newspapers identifying where dignitaries and people of influence were gathering, and our movement would then gather outside and hold our silent protests.

It was 1976, and my son Matthew was born of love, but I quickly discovered that you cannot live on love alone. This was a big wake-up call for me. If I had been a welder, I would have had a trade to earn a living. But turning up at interviews to state my only qualification was that of a Hippie, who incidentally could pull a mighty pint, didn't quite cut the mustard.

And so, my difficult life began – I had to learn how to support a family in a strange country knowing only my wife's parents and siblings. I struggled and failed, which ended my marriage. I now had a son living in America and, though it did go through my head to return to England, I couldn't leave him, even if I was on the outskirts of his life watching him grow by paying alimony only. The magnitude of mental and emotional pain I went through pushed me into depression. All of this pain I meticulously scrutinized as I tried to understand the 'why' and the 'what' of the choices I had made, resulting in a painful lonely existence interspersed by glimpses of love with my child. I slowly slipped into my 'dark night of the soul.'

Pauline also was suffering domestic violence in New Zealand, and she too travelled 'the dark night of the soul.' We corresponded, supported each other, and shared the lessons that were played out before us. We dug deep into our souls and would point out what the other couldn't see. But when it became clear that either one of us needed specialist help, we would point the other in that direction.

We both recognized through our interaction the irony of our lives. Both firm activists of Peace and our lives were anything but!

Mum visits America to meet Matthew. 1st June 1978

1983 onward
My time with David Guardino

Walter

My ex-wife did have a caring family and they were extremely supportive of me. I particularly enjoyed my time with her father who was a lovely, honest churchgoing man. Her brother became a friend and had started a business as a 'Psychic to the Stars' no less! I did like him as a person and when he asked me if I would go to work for him in a general capacity around his big new house it was easy for me to say yes. I would learn a lot, he promised, and I did! Perhaps not in the way he intended as he woke me up to the 'business of making money' on a large scale.

He obtained an exceptionally large house in Las Vegas which allowed room for me to escape the constant chatter of CNN Headline News. This played in his world night and day, as he had to absorb it. He had to keep up with the play to enable him to deliver the right sort of psychic responses to his customer base – the stars!

Working for David was more like being an indentured servant than an employee. If I asked for a day off, he would complain that he had to work every day so why shouldn't I?

David had converted one of the rooms into an office. He worked night and day, often falling asleep while holding the phone to his ear. Everyone in the house would answer the phone and take down the name and number of the caller; David would then phone the prospective client back and reel them in. The small fish, the ones that could only afford to send him a hundred dollars, never heard from him again. They would call and complain that he no longer spoke to them. We would tell them that David was terribly busy. We assured them that he was working extremely hard on their behalf and recommended that they write a letter. The big fish, the ones that paid his asking fee of $10,000 received ongoing attention, mainly because he continued to get more money out of them.

An extraordinarily rich woman who inherited property in Florida would come to Las Vegas to meet with David at a high-priced restaurant. David would drink the best wine and eat the best food, at her expense, while trying to wheedle more money out of her. She had more money than most people could even dream of, but what she wanted was a lover.

The woman was very plain. Some might even say she was ugly, and she hired David to bring love and romance into her life. During one of her visits, David asked me if I would sleep with her. My look of horror told him the answer, but then he said he would pay me $500 to do so. It was the age of free love, so I had no qualms about the morality of sleeping with a strange woman, and the prospect of being paid to do so did not violate my standard of ethics.

David's wife took me shopping for new clothes that would fit the criteria of an English aristocrat. Up until this time, I was still wearing my Hippie clothes. She insisted I had a haircut to complete the look and play the part properly, so I was remodeled and didn't even recognize myself when I stepped out!

Suitably adorned in my finery, I was told where to meet the client. We had a few drinks, and I needed every one of them, before going to her room at the MGM Grand.

I did my duty, but what she wanted was to talk. We ordered wine from room service, and I soon found her to be a highly intelligent woman with a charming personality. We sipped fine wine and talked through the night. She told me she often paid to have sex with movie stars, and one of her favorites was Dan Haggerty who had short-lived fame playing the role of Grizzly Adams on television.

The next morning David met with her for breakfast. Upon returning home with a huge smile on his face, he gave me $500. I didn't ask how much he had charged her for my services, but by the look on his face, I'm sure it was a lot more than he gave me. The feedback I received was that she would like my services regularly in the future, through Psychic to the Stars of course.

David was now into a real money maker with me being his 'stud' that he could hire out and began working on my promotion within his business.

On one of my 'jobs' accompanied by David, I was taken to meet his client at a French Restaurant, and to my amazement, she had her husband with her. She had been a nurse before her husband paid her way through medical school and now both of them were doctors. I couldn't believe my luck; she was stunningly beautiful. Her problem was that her husband was sexually impotent, and in a very discreet way, she wanted to satisfy her natural desires. I felt very awkward during dinner, but her husband noticed my discomfort and put me at ease with a smile on his face and in his eyes. It was one of the strangest experiences of my life. After we had eaten, I made polite conversation with the doctors. We sipped expensive wine while David, sporting a big white bib around his neck, seemed to be chugging it back by the bottles. A waiter hovered next to the table awaiting our every whim.

It all looked perfectly normal. All the rules of polite society were followed, but as we spoke and exchanged smiles, I couldn't forget the fact that when we left the dinner table the husband would give his wife a small kiss, and then, with his full blessing, his beautiful wife and I would be going to a room where we strip naked and enjoy wild, and very passionate sex. To the waiter, we probably appeared to be very casual, but each word we spoke, and every glance, was measured!

The experience gave me a whole new understanding of the word 'sophistication'. I realized that I was amongst a different class of people, and they were a lot different from the British working class into which I had been born and raised. I felt like a veil of ignorance was slipping from my eyes, and I congratulated myself on becoming wise to the ways of the world. The various women that paid for my 'services' became my regulars (what a life!)

But as I entered into what I assumed to be the 'real' world; David slowly descended into a fantasy world of his own making. He slept for only one or two hours a night, and the lack of sleep was slowly taking its toll on his body and mind. He boasted that he would soon be the richest man in the world, and he was definitely making a lot of money, but he never had the chance to enjoy it. His world was a 10 x 15-foot office, and in that world, he could be anything he wanted to be. He had an amazing brain and with it, he created a world of lies and deceit, and in his world, he was – The Psychic to the Stars.

It didn't help matters when a lot of very respectable people encouraged him along his path to insanity by paying him $10,000 to tell them what they wanted to hear.

I knew things were getting serious when he started to refer to his father, the honest churchgoing Monte Guardino, as the 'Godfather.' Somehow, in his deluded and sleep-deprived mind, David concluded that his Sicilian descent, his Italian name, and the fact that he was rich and living in Las Vegas could only mean one thing, the mafia; if he were to be in the mafia then his father must be the boss of bosses. As such, good old God-fearing Monte was then transformed, in David's mind, into 'The Godfather.'

My assuredness that I had David all figured out experienced a severe challenge when Richard Bryan, the Governor of Nevada, with his entourage, showed up at David's door. The Governor was shown into David's office where he stayed for over an hour. His bodyguards gave me serious looks, daring me to make a wrong move, while his assistants made phone calls and wrote things in leather-bound notebooks. His visit came as a total surprise to me. The Governor was expected by David, but his visit had to be shrouded in secrecy. It seemed odd that the Governor came to David rather than telling David to come to him, and the visit was obviously about something that couldn't be discussed over the phone.

To this day, I still don't know what the Governor of Nevada and David Guardino talked about. I guess that it had something to do with UFOs around Roswell Air Force Base (we'd heard at the time). After serving as Governor, Richard Bryan went on to serve Nevada in the US Senate, where he single-handedly managed to kill NASA's SETI project for the scientific search for extraterrestrial civilizations against the opinion of thousands of scientists, including Dr Carl Sagan and several Nobel Prize winners.

"The Great Martian Chase," he said "may finally come to an end. As of today, millions have been spent and we have yet to bag a single little green person. Not a single Martian has said 'take me to your leader' and not a single flying saucer has applied for FAA approval."

Why did Richard Bryan spend so much time and energy stopping the search for extraterrestrial life? And if he was such a sceptic, then why was he talking to Dave Guardino, a professed psychic, for over an hour? David never said a word about the meeting before or after it.

Another event that forced me to reassess David was when David Letterman decided to call him live on his nationwide *Late Night with David Letterman* television show. David G had to be told to expect the phone call, and he and his wife and I sat in the living room watching the show as Letterman led up to the phone call. He said that he noticed David's advertisement and he was going to call David Guardino to ask him a few questions about his dubious psychic abilities. He told his assistant to make the call. David stared with a stone-cold face at the television screen as we listened to the numbers being dialled. The connection was made, and we heard the phone ring, but then came the sound of static. Letterman told his assistant to dial again. The sound of the numbers being dialled was heard yet again, but once again the call failed and all we could hear on the television was static.

I looked at David. He was motionless and as cold looking as marble. Letterman, meanwhile, was growing increasingly agitated. He demanded to know why his assistant could not even complete a simple phone call. After one more try, he gave up, but he promised his viewers that he would try again at another time.

The next time came a week later. David G was notified and was just as stone-faced as he was at the earlier call. And the results were just the same as they were the previous week. On the television, Letterman was visibly angry at his staff as he gave up on the call. David, without saying a word about it, got up from his chair and went back into his office to resume making money.

Federal Judge Harry Eugene Clairborne was the fifth person in US History to be removed from public office through impeachment. He was first indicted by a federal grand jury for bribery, fraud, and tax evasion in December of 1983. Shortly after that, he called David Guardino.

Former Clark County District Attorney George Dickerson said about him, "Harry Clairborne was, without doubt, the greatest criminal defense attorney in the southwest United States." Many attorneys said his skills in a courtroom were unparalleled in the state's history, with some saying even that was an understatement. He was appointed to be a federal judge for the U.S. District Court for the District of Nevada by President Jimmy Carter in 1978.

One cannot deny that Harry Clairborne was an extremely intelligent man who was well-educated in the ways of the world. Yet when he got indicted, he decided to call on David Guardino to influence others to do his bidding.

David decided to throw a dinner party in Clairborne's honour. To make a good impression he asked me to pretend to be his English butler. I was fitted out in tails, striped pants, and a bow tie to look the part. On the night of the dinner party, I opened the front door to welcome the guests. Then with my best imitation of a posh British accent, I would ask them to please walk this way. When I opened the door to Harry Clairborne, he mistook me for the host and congratulated me on how fit I looked. With a calm gaze and a stiff upper lip, I replied, "Sir, Mister Guardino is awaiting your arrival in the dining room."

He followed me to the dining room to find a very overweight Mister Guardino clad in a gaudy red and white tracksuit. As dinner progressed, I stood by the dining room door looking serious and haughty as the maids brought out the food and refilled the wine glasses. The wine flowed like a river. After they had eaten, Judge Clairborne stood to give an after-dinner speech. He was famous for his articulate storytelling abilities that captivated jurors. Senior U.S. District Judge Lloyd George said of him: "He could tell a story better than anyone I've ever known." And on that night Judge Clairborne lived up to his reputation. He was brilliant. His sense of humour was outrageous, and the dining room was soon filled with laughter. He was better than any stand-up comedian I had ever heard, and I had a tough time keeping my face straight.

He told of a rape trial where he asked the victim if the man had penetrated her, and after a short pause, while she thought about it, she replied, "It certainly felt like it went right through me," I could hold it no longer and the pent-up laughter exploded out of me. Judge Clairborne looked my way, and then, with an amused expression in his eyes, he seemed to say, "So you're supposed to be an English butler, eh?"

I don't know whether it was because of David's psychic influence but in April 1984 the jury deadlocked, and a mistrial was declared. But the judge was tried again in July on only tax evasion charges and was found guilty the next month, thus becoming the first federal judge ever convicted of crimes while on the bench. He was sentenced to two years in prison. He was impeached by the U.S. House of Representatives on July 22, 1986, and was convicted by the U.S. Senate on October 9, 1986, removing him from office. Clairborne continued to profess his innocence right up to January 2004 when he fatally shot himself in Las Vegas.

My escape from death

Working for David didn't pay a great deal, but it wasn't arduous work. He paid for my clothes; I had no worries about utility bills or making rent payments. My child support was being paid each month (to his sister!) and I was never without a bed, a meal, or entertainment. But it all nearly came to a tragic end after I made the mistake of accusing a maid, the one who made my bed, of stealing from my jar of quarters. I kept putting quarters in the jar, but the jar kept getting emptier. It had to be her because the maid was the only other person that entered my room, and she was taking them out faster than I was putting them in. David's wife and the maid were friends so I decided to tell her about the situation in the hope that she would tell the maid to stop. The maid denied it and she threatened to put a voodoo curse on me if I continued to make the charges. Her threat didn't scare me. I ridiculed her belief in voodoo and told her to go ahead with the curse but to stop taking my quarters.

A few days later, I awoke with a large painful discolouration on my right thigh. As the morning progressed, the discolouration turned into a nasty-looking lump that kept growing bigger. I began to feel nauseous; my head throbbed with pain; my face was drained of blood, and I began to think I was dying. I was trying to work but had to tell David's wife that I must go back to bed. She looked at me in a strange state of alarm and told me to go back into my bedroom as she needed to see this. Once there she told me to pull my pants down, took one look at the discoloured lump on my thigh, and said, "Come on, you're going to the hospital."

David's wife was also friends with one of the doctors at the hospital. He was often at the house for dinner, and when we arrived at the emergency room, he was waiting for me at the door. He showed me into a room, took one look at the lump, and said, "You've been bitten by a Brown Recluse spider," and then injected me with the antidote.

As I lay in bed recovering, I couldn't help but marvel at my luck. The Brown Recluse is the deadliest spider in America, and if not for the prompt actions of David's wife I might have died. But then I began to wonder why she looked so alarmed when she told me to go into the bedroom. Why was the doctor waiting for me at the emergency room door? And why didn't I go through the usual procedure of giving my name to the admissions office? I didn't give my name to anyone! And how come the doctors had the antidote so close at hand? Had he tried to tell me something when he asked me if I had been in any small dirty places?

"It's called recluse because it likes to hide," he said. There was only one answer – the maid had tried and failed with the voodoo curse, so she decided to place a Brown Recluse spider between my sheets instead. For some reason, she must have had a change of heart and decided to confess her actions to David's wife who, before asking me to pull my pants down to inspect my lump, she must have phoned her doctor friend at the hospital telling him about the Brown Recluse bite, and that's why I bypassed the paperwork at the hospital. It all made perfect sense now.

From that day on, I was always nice to David's chambermaids. I never even checked my quarter jar again. I kept putting the quarters in, but I don't remember thinking about taking one out. In the world that David lived in, everyone was on the take, and I learned the hard way that sometimes the wisest course of action was to just let them take it.

But David started to take a bit too much when he began to use the credit card numbers of his clients without their permission, and he grew increasingly paranoid after getting word that the FBI was investigating him. The paranoia only made his mental state worse, and he became increasingly more difficult to be around. One day, the parents of a missing child came to the house. David said he could help for a fee. I looked at their sad faces. Then I looked at David's pudgy, bloated face from living his high life, and I knew my time working for him was ending.

The end came shortly after I invited a beautiful Asian woman over for dinner. I met her at the supermarket. She noticed that I bought the huge roast beef that was on display in the meat department. She followed me to the parking lot and saw me go to the immaculate Lincoln Town Car. She must have thought I was a rich man, so she struck up a conversation with me. I invited her over to help eat the roast beef, and when she arrived at the house David became exceedingly jealous. After dinner, the woman and I went to my room. When she left, David stormed into my room screaming, "This house is not a brothel!"

The next morning upon my request, the maid called a taxi for me. When the taxi arrived, I went into David's office and told him I was quitting. He responded, "Nobody quits on David Guardino!" and then pulled a gun on me. I doubted that he would pull the trigger. I figured he would be too afraid of what Monte the Godfather would say about it. So, I turned my back on David, praying my gut instinct was correct, and whether or not he was scared of what his father might say. The main thing is he didn't pull the trigger. So, I said goodbye to the maid and David's wife and walked out the front door to the waiting taxi.

Shortly after I quit working for him, the FBI closed in on David. Eventually, he went to prison for credit card theft.

A few years after he was released from jail, I was sitting at home flipping through the TV channels when I came to a boxing match and decided to watch it. When the bell rang for the end of the round, much to my astonishment, David Guardino clambered up to the corner of one of the fighters. He didn't say anything, just stood there in silence. When the bell rang to resume the fight, he sat back down again. The same thing happened at the end of every round. The fighter had paid David to influence the fight by being there in his corner. And luckily for David, his client won.

While working for David, I almost got into trouble with the law in Tennessee, but I didn't. I almost died from the Brown Recluse spider bite in Las Vegas, but I didn't. I almost got entangled in an FBI investigation, but I didn't, and I almost got shot, but I didn't. What I got was an education in the ways of the real world – and I got to legally stay in America.

David's mother and sister (my ex-wife) wrote a book about David's life and called it *The Psychic to the Stars*. His mother never gave up hope for him and when he died, she was convinced he would be residing in heaven. I would like to think that Harry Clairborne is there too and that Harry is telling David one of his funny stories. Nobody is all bad, and nobody is all good, and when it all comes down to dust: David did not have an easy life. He was often betrayed by those he trusted. He was an addict, and most of his life was spent trying to find his daily fix. He was addicted to money, and in the end, he died a pauper's death. David finished up a big-time loser, but if it turns out that David Guardino came out of it all as a big-time winner, then that's all right by me.

My second child Sarah

Walter

I went on to marry for a second time and had a daughter that we called Sarah. She was born in 1987 exactly eleven years after my son and she arrived on the same date. (Was this an omen?) Again, that marriage didn't last.

Fear

It's the end of January 1999 and the end of the nightmare we've been living through: Sarah's heart murmur and leakage. The operations are over and she is completely cured. Everyone was shocked to hear she had a heart condition; she is so gung-ho. Well, now she's gone and gung-hoed the heart condition as well. This kid is a Hicks! She's living with me now and her Mum has gone off to Texas. We have our yelling matches though – she's eleven now, going on teenager from hell and we battle now and then for control, but I always win because I'm bigger. However, I still haven't figured out how come she always gets her way in the end!

I was living in a state of fear, wound up like a tight spring yet not aware I was living like this. Then once Sarah received the all-clear, as I unwound a little more each day, only then did I realise how I had been living. Dad's words came back to me.

I could have been about eighteen or nineteen years old but don't know what age I was when he said this. However, I've never forgotten it. "You're scared!" he said. His neck was red and his whole face seemed puffed up. Judging by the ferocity of his gaze and the contempt in his eyes, I felt like I was the scum of the universe. I looked him in the eye and didn't say a word. How could I lie to such a fierce stare? He was right. I was scared.

He glared back at me and said, "Think of someone else for a change."

That was it. But I've carried it with me to this day. I'd never achieved it. That is, not until I saw Sarah through two heart operations. For the first time in my life, I did think of someone else instead of myself and I put that person ahead of myself even to the point of death.

Pauline

When I was frightened of Dad and his explosions of anger after whisky drink, I held you and Johnson when you were babies, and me soothing you both helped me. Then you became a teenager and I remember a night of Dad's wild anger in Corporation Road and my bedroom door opened and your head popped around it saying, "Are you okay?" You knew how much fear I would be feeling. I was sitting on my bed dressed ready to run if he came into my room (which he never did, but I always prepared myself as this was part of my fear.) You hugged me and comforted me saying, "He never climbs stairs when he's this drunk so you'll be okay. I'm leaving my bedroom door open and will confront him if he does. I'll put him to bed." So, you did achieve it, Walt. I remember that night and your thinking of me and wrapping your arms around me.

Pauline & Babs's first meeting with Sarah

Sarah with her Daddy

Walter and Pauline philosophizing

Walter

Thomas Merton, the Trappist monk and sometimes hermit, wrote: *At any given time in the history of the world there are only two or three people who are totally free of illusion, and these people are, in a way, holding up the universe.*

Then think about this one – W.B Yeats wrote in his diary: *All civilization is held together by the suggestion of an invisible hypnotist – by artificially created illusions. The knowledge of reality is always in some measure a secret knowledge. It is a kind of death.*

Let's face it, we are all deluded, and we all have our favourite illusions. The two or three people (at any one time on earth) that Thomas Merton talks about that aren't deluded are probably living in caves on top of a mountain to get away from us lot!

It's not breaking news either. Just read any of the great philosophers, poets, and/or writers and what is it that they are looking for? Bloody reality, that's what!

The condition begins at birth when we somehow get the silly feeling that we are the centre of the universe. Then as growing children, we find out about pretence and the joy of playing.

As parents, we find nothing wrong with the child at the door asking if Johnny can come out to play. But be warned, the innocent-looking wee one might be an agent for the invisible hypnotist.

Just look at the facts. As children, we play and pretend for fun. Then, as adolescents, we begin to play and pretend for real. If there's anything left of our true self after all the pretence in childhood it is soon disintegrated by peer pressure, sex hormones, and intense pressure from adults who want us to conform to society's norm. If we ever get through adolescence, we then become fully functioning *deluded* adults and role models for our children no less!

We continue on the journey until we've raised our fully functioning deluded kids, then we decide not to be deluded anymore. This condition is called post-mid-life crisis.

If we survive the mid-life crisis, we are determined to no longer live by the rules of such a screwed-up world. We finally get tired of the pretence and it's suddenly time for truth, and the best way to find the truth seems to be in the telling of it. So, we become what's called cranky old buggers and hypocrites. Then shortly after that we die.

I mean – there you go!

For all we know, the two or three that Merton talks about, the sane ones that live in reality, may be locked up in an insane asylum. All this talk in Quantum Mechanics about parallel worlds and such, I mean, it may well be true.

But nothing seems to exist without an opposite, and it's obvious to me that the opposite world to this one must be the sane one.

(We speculated on this subject over many pages and much time.)

Pauline

One of my statements following.

The Human 'Race'

Instructions for emerging adults

You will wake up each morning and paint on your face.
Don your clean tracksuit and enter 'the race.'
This race we call 'time' –we're not sure yet for what?
It's time to spend! with what? … we haven't yet got!

My questions
If a traveller falls
Must we leave them behind?
Can we stop to give aid?
Is there time to be 'kind'?
Do we know where we're going?
Will we ever get there?
Can we have dreams?
Does anyone care?

The rules are.
Conform to society – it means race – like the rest.
Fall away breathless – and you've failed the test
Be individual – and we'll label you mad.
Be quiet and withdrawn – and for you we'll feel sad.

My response
But no one wants pity!
And no one wants scorn!
So **when** can we be
Just the way we were born?

Princess Diana 1997

Walter

As you know, I walked out of my job in the factory as it was killing my soul. It was worse than Cammell Lairds. I had sure faith that I would revive and be reborn. All I had to do was to get the fuck out of there. I've had a month off and I am slowly coming back to life. *My life* – me living with *'Me.'* Then Princess Diana was killed. Where does this fit into my life thoughts? I pondered this as I watched the TV screens and rattled my brain to make some sense of why she had to die.

When someone dies it seems like the energy that they were is released to the world. Things reveal themselves upon the leaving. And none of us knew the energy that Diana had until she left. Her brother spoke like a true nobleman at her funeral, and he criticized the press for always questioning her motives. He said, "Maybe it's because genuine goodness is threatening to those at the other end of the spectrum."

I was astounded at the sincere feelings of the English. Where there is mourning there can't be falseness. The mask of society is dropped at that time and the mourners fall back, in a way, nearer to their true sense of being. There are no pretenses amongst the grief-stricken. The house of mourning is the one that has the 'truth' in it.

I was struck by the contrast between the Royal family, with all their pomp and ceremony, and this vivacious, wonderful, caring, fully alive being that they rejected. The Royal family, whose whole life is an act, rejected the living truth of Diana. Diana was closer to the real state of Being, and I suppose her true Being and their act clashed. As a result, Diana died.

But the act and the illusion in England didn't win. In her death, and by the energy that she released in her death, she won. She wasn't a real princess anymore, but the people said that she was, and the Royals had to finally listen to the people. She became the People's Princess.

I have had many a bitter thought toward the English and being an Irishman, I think I've had worthy cause for doing so. But after watching this funeral, with the streets drenched in tears and covered in flowers, I could feel my heart reach out to this sad Nation. I could feel their grief, and I could see their sincerity and their remorse as they finally got a sense of the 'truth' that comes from loss. I marveled at the sight of them, the stiff-upper-lipped Englishmen, actually crying in the streets. I felt all the anger and hatred that I had held towards them evaporate, and I could only feel compassion for this sad old enemy.

I thought at first that I could feel my heart make peace with this nation of conquerors, as they lamented a loss, and as they mourned for their princess, the princess of the outcasts and the lowly, The Queen of Hearts. However, after some thinking, I found that the peace I was making was not with the English – I've never really hated them as individuals – I just hated them for what they stood for. I hate their attitude of superiority and I detest their class system. But what I was making peace with was something more profound than the feeling of understanding with a deluded race of people. I found that I was surrendering and making peace with the feminine part of the world, and with the feminine part of myself.

I don't mean sex; sex has nothing to do with what I'm thinking. I'm talking about the expression of my being and the acknowledgment of an emotion.

Many women are not feminine. The so-called women libbers

are coming from the masculine part of their being more than most men are. It is not a feminine thing to abort a child so that it won't interfere with your life. Some women are aggressive and self-serving and seem to resent the fact that they are women.

The feminine that I'm talking about is the sense of acceptance, the sense of surrender to the circumstances, the sense of compassion, and the understanding that gives rise to a nurturing spirit that's willing to sacrifice everything for the wellbeing of another.

I don't know much about religion, but I think that the sense of loss and the mourning for Diana was like a religious experience for the spiritually starved people of England.

Within days of the death of Diana, I heard that Mother Theresa of Calcutta had died. Two great feminine women dying in the same week is a bit of a coincidence. And, as I don't believe in coincidence, I conclude this must be an omen. This is a huge release of powerful female energy.

The press made a big deal out of it when Diana took off her glove and then shook hands with a man who was stricken with AIDS. But if it were Mother Theresa doing it, it wouldn't have been newsworthy. Diana came from a position of privilege and told us that we are all the same. She used her position to help those with no privilege at all, those that pay for society's ways with their life as they rot away in the ghetto.

Mother Theresa said that we are all the same and she did more than shake hands with the downtrodden and infectious, she lived with them and died with them. She rolled up her sleeves and went to work. She held them in her arms, and then she went out into the streets and found more of them lying in the gutters and took them to a place where they could die with dignity, and she also gave them a bit of hope too.

They were both great women and it doesn't matter which one saved the most lives and gave the most comfort to the rejected ones that society considers worthless. I think that they both came from the same place and gave from the heart. Maybe they both had a preordained job to do, and it appears that they both did it extremely well.

But there were no tears in England for Mother Theresa. She just wasn't newsworthy. She wasn't beautiful in the physical sense. She was old, frail, and looked haggard. No rich powerful men were wanting to marry her. In death, she took a humble second place, that is, according to the newspapers and the propagandists that we call the media. Newspapers must be sold to make a profit. On the TV the news needs sponsors. What has the truth got to do with it? But I'm sure that it's not going to bother Mother Theresa. If she's in heaven, that she appeared to believe in with such certainty, then she's happy. If she's not and she's just dead, then what does it matter? It's not going to hurt her either way.

Something strange is happening in the world, and something strange is happening to me. I've been thinking about spending a weekend in a monastery. Tell me about your experiences when you have done that. I'm also thinking about going to church this coming Sunday. I might have been wrong in my opinion of organized religion. Not that I ever really had an opinion, my mind was set for me by my forebearers and by the ravaging of my class during the industrial revolution. I just picked up the attitude and ran with it. I've always thought religion was just a tool that the state used to keep us in servitude. But who knows?

I think that I've been wrong about almost everything in my life. All that I've believed in has turned out to be false. If I have any sanity left to keep, then I must believe that the sanest thing is to admit that I've been wrong about everything.

I've read somewhere that there is no silence unless it's shared silence, and I wouldn't mind experiencing and sharing that silence that the monks have for a wee while.

Sometimes a molehill is a mountain to me, and what's a

matchstick to others is an impassable barrier for me to climb over. I think it's good to realize that about myself. Surely, we are all the same! We all have an impassable barrier that appears as a matchstick to others, and we must all see a mountain in our own eyes where it's only a molehill to those sitting on it.

I might be a daft Irishman, but I'm not so daft as to believe in what passes for reality in this strange and deluded world. How can any of us from the lowest to the highest, from the so-called commoner to the so-called elite, claim that we have a handle on reality? What is worse than having a deluded being force his delusion on a child? Is one mask any worse than any other? Are we all deluded? Are we all living in denial? Are we all daft? Is this a world of the deluded? It's been called a ship of fools, and I believe it.

I'm a fool all right, but I believe in this world like I believe that I was found under a cabbage patch.

Pauline

Reality for me is individual and still a personal choice. Let me explain it in a story that I placed in my Perils of Pauline book.

I employed two car painters on a month's trial and kept one at the end of that month because he could do twice as much work as the other.

Every Monday morning, I would give these two men the same amount of work to do for the week. By Wednesday or Thursday one of them would be in the office looking for more work and the other struggled every Friday afternoon to finish his original tasks.

Each time I opened my office door and looked into the workshop one of them was moving around the workshop at the speed of light. The other always seemed to be standing staring at his work. This sight amused me. I felt as though I'd employed a pinball machine and a statue.

At the end of the month, I let him go. I sacked the pinball

machine.

Each Monday morning that I had employed this man he stood before me and with each job I gave him I could see his mind kicking into action. By the time he had left my office, this man had his mind set to 'very busy.' Because he was 'very busy' his mistakes were supposed to be an accepted part of his work. His life energy was sucked into his mind and used up by the *thought* of being 'very busy.' Tools would be left all over the shop and when he needed them for the next job he never knew where he had left them as he raced around trying to find them. The bake oven (an expensive piece of equipment) was switched on and off, on and off, all day long. At the end of each day, this man was exhausted.

The statue was given his list of jobs and in contrast, he would walk into the workshop with an open mind to work out the best way of going about his duties. He looked at each job carefully and worked out what part of each he could do while using the same tool. He earmarked the bake oven for himself on Wednesday morning and Friday morning and the pinball machine was grateful because **he** used it for the rest of the week. The statue was a pleasure to talk to. I learned all about his family and the quality time he had with them when he finished his day's work. The pinball had no time to talk and went to the pub after work because he needed to unwind. The statue was refreshed and ready to enjoy his family life after work and the pinball machine was 'done in.'

Each of these men had the same working day, the same workload, and the same work environment. But if you were to ask each of these men how their day was, you would get two completely different descriptions.

Each of these men, just like every one of us on this earth, creates their own reality.

The mind is the most powerful tool we have. It is our personal computer. Each morning you wake and on opening your eyes you have pressed the on button. Your life to date has been carefully programmed into your hard drive, the thoughts you work by, and your patterns of behaviour. The mistake that most people make is in thinking that the automated mind is who they are. Rather than using the mind as a tool, most people let the mind use them. This personal computer is then in control of their lives. Because most people never learn how to use it efficiently, they open their eyes in the morning and hey!! They are away!! The computer says I must do this, the computer says I must do that. When you use the computer at your desk you can have more than one program open at any one time - yes? Well, that's exactly how some people's mind computer is. They work on this job as they think about the next job, as they think of what to eat for dinner, as they think of how to help little Johnny to do his homework tonight, as they think of this weekend and how lovely it will be not to be working. All these programs are running at the same time. At the end of the day, you ask these people about their day and they say *I'm exhausted; it was hectic*!!! Was the day hectic? or the way they thought about the day? The day was the same day for you as it was for me. There were eight hours in that working day, did you enjoy each of those hours doing something productive that you are good at? If you stay in the NOW freshly facing each challenge, each job is getting the attention it deserves and you can create the best that you can for each project.

Everything in NOW is fresh and new and for the first time. Did you miss that hinted offer of a fantastic job because your mind wasn't truly in the NOW so you weren't paying attention to the person talking to you? Did you miss the first time of something pleasurable because you were in yesterday or tomorrow? Did you miss your baby's smile because your mind was on other things? Did you miss the way that old couple looked at each other, smiled, and then held hands? Did you miss that bird singing its little heart out this morning to welcome you into the day? Did you miss the sunrise or sunset all because your mind was either in the past or the future and programmed for 'very busy'?

It is not easy to stop the internal chatter of these computer programs when you have never done it before but it is worth learning. The absolute best advice I can give to anyone is to learn to meditate. Buy a book on 'how to' or download an app on your phone or join a class.

We have been raised hearing that 'life' can be hard. I disagree – "*LIFE*" is the purest, simplest, most uncomplicated energy – it is what our minds do with it that causes the pain and confusion and makes it hard.

The statue painter used his life energy and personal mind computer wisely and was in control of his energy with the right balance of his foot on the accelerator. The pinball machine painter allowed his personal mind computer to use his life energy, and it alone dominated the accelerator as it used up his energy.

Each of these men had the same resources and tools and yet each created a very different reality.

The Sioux Indians have a quote that says it all so simply.

The Creator gathered all of creation together and said "I want to hide something from humans until each of them, individually, is ready for it. It is the realization that "They create their own Reality."

The eagle said, "Give it to me, and I will take it to the moon."

The Creator said, "No, one day collectively, they will go there and find it."

The salmon said, "I will hide it at the bottom of the Ocean."

The Creator said, "No, they will go there too."

The buffalo said, "I will bury it on the great plains."

"No," The Creator said. "They will cut into the skin of the earth and find it even there."

Then Wise Old Grandmother Mole, who lives in the breast of Mother Earth and who has no eyes, but 'sees' said, "Put it inside them," and the Creator said, "It is done."

An immensely proud Dad with his kids

Sarah with her dad ready for her brother's wedding

We philosophized over the ego for some time. Following is a snapshot.

Pauline November 1997

As I was eating my breakfast and thinking of what we are discussing – to help me identify the ego, I can explain it as hats that I wear. If you can put a title to it then the ego is needed to enable you to perform in the manufactured world that we have created. Each hat has a title on it – now I am Mother, now I am daughter, now I am teacher, now I am taxi driver, now I am whatever! This is the fabricated world and we need the ego to work in that world we've created. Our daily hats (bread).

When you are sitting staring across blue waters or walking in the woods – the natural world – then you put the ego to one side (transcend it) and allow the spirit to skip and play in its natural environment.

Your worries in this world are observed through you by your ego – your mind remembers it and waits for the appropriate moment when the ego is out of the way and then delivers it to 'spirit' to sort out. The answer comes to you as in a blinding revelation. Spirit has done its work! A walk in the woods – bingo – the answer to a problem arises. Disconnect from the ego, sit in meditation, and the answers to our problems can be revealed to us. Meditation is practice at sitting in the spirit world. No connection to ego – complete freedom from worldly woes. Spending some time there (20 minutes meditation) is the equivalent of a colonic irrigation (sorry about that but I was looking for a powerful cleansing medium) we have washed out the toxic waste and spirit can now work better with a clear path.

Walter

That's a good way of looking at it. My old dictionary from 1958 describes the ego as: *I; the whole person; self; the personal identity*. If we see the ego in this way then to overcome one's ego means to overcome oneself. The traditional way of doing this, I would think, is to give oneself to God through religion. Overcoming one's ego in this way is to give it away to a higher power and thus serve the higher power rather than one's ego. This works in theory but hardly ever works in practice. Most people who give themselves to a higher power end up wanting the higher power to serve their ego. This is evident in their prayers for a car or a winning lottery ticket. It's most evident in wars where it's been said that there are no atheists in foxholes.

Also, the majority of converts to religion are in dire need of being saved from themselves or their Karma, and the American Christian fundamentalist of being born again is very popular in prisons be they of a physical or mental structure.

Like you, I have difficulty in giving my ego away to a religion that seems to have lost its way and doesn't seem to be in touch with its roots anymore. I see Christianity in that way, and that's why I'm no longer a member of a church. I almost laughed with disdain when I heard the Pope bemoan the fate of the poor while wearing a diamond-studded gown no less. Jesus would have kicked him off the podium. But I don't want to put anyone down; there are a lot of good people in all religions, and they are serving a purpose by giving hope to those that cannot see their way forward. Plus, it's a waste of time being negative. Suffice it to say that I have seen the light.

Jesus and Buddha were super strong people with huge egos. They were so powerful that they felt strong enough to attack the established religion in the places and times where they were born. Jesus verbally attacked Judaism and Buddha attacked Hinduism. Both preached the same basic message of 'love thy neighbour like thyself' but the thing that strikes me the most is that both were very humble. They were strong, and to us, they might even be egotistic, one could even say supernaturally so, but one could also say they in paradox were ego-less people. They were humble because they knew that the Power they were exhibiting came from somewhere else and worked through them. The Power came from the unity they had made with the infinite divine nature of 'Being' which is better known as God. They plugged into the One-ness of Being. Maybe when Jesus said: "My father and I are one" or 'Why do you call me good? Only the Father is good" or "Do unto others as you would have them do unto you' just maybe he was talking about the One-ness that the Buddha, and now Quantum Mechanics, talks about.

Acceptance is one of the things we need to do right off the bat. There is no way of changing or escaping from karma unless we admit we are serving time in one. It's simple cause and effect, or cause and karma, or karma and what the hell do we do now? Freedom is linked with responsibility. One could even say there is no freedom without responsibility, and when we take responsibility for our karma we also miraculously get the truth that will enable us to find the Power to overcome it. 'The truth can set us free!' but it's certainly not in churches, the truth can only be found between our individually owned ears; which in a way is another paradox; we are all one, but we can only find out about our truth individually and on our own. Ultimately, it all comes down, or up, to our own egos. Only we, as an ego, can decide to turn the light of truth on or off.

We have the freedom of choice. When we were young, we had no choice but to believe what we were told, but we have survived to a place where we can now decide for ourselves about what is true and what is not.

In Buddhism, it is believed that we choose our parents. We choose for the spiritual lessons we will get from them. We choose our parents for the challenges they offer us. If this is true then it's no wonder that we have ended up in the same library. We started in the same place, we went over the road to Birkenhead Library, and here we are again in a completely different library. As Tommy

Cooper would say "Just like that!" Or as Dad's favourite comedian, Harry Worth, would say "I don't know Why?"

Love yer – keep it coming, **Walt**!

Pauline

Ken Wilber is my guru as you know – and I have uncovered his thoughts on the ego.

Ken Wilber – Transformations of Consciousness

All the things that people typically have trouble with – money, food, sex, relationships, desire, – they want their saints to be without. Egoless sages are above all that, is what people want. Talking heads is what they want. Religion, they believe, will simply get rid of all the baser instincts, drives, and relationships, and hence they look to religion, not for advice on how to live life with enthusiasm, but on how to avoid it, repress it, deny it, and escape it.

In other words, the typical person wants the spiritual sage to be 'less than a person,' somehow devoid of all the messy, juicy, complex, pulsating, desiring, urging forces that drive most human beings. We expect our sages to be an absence of all that drives us! All the things that frighten us, confuse us, torment us, confound us: we want our sages to be untouched by them altogether. And that absence, that vacancy, that 'less than personal', is what we often mean by 'egoless'.

But 'egoless', does not mean 'less than personal', it means 'more than personal'. Not personal minus, but personal PLUS – all the normal personal qualities, PLUS some transpersonal ones. Think of the great yogis, saints, and sages – from Moses to Christ to Padmasambhava. They were not feeble-mannered milquetoasts, but fierce movers and shakers – from wielding bullwhips in the Temple to subduing entire countries. They rattled the world on its terms, not in some pie-in-the-sky piety; many of them instigated massive social revolutions that have continued for thousands of years. And they did so, not because they avoided the physical, emotional, and mental dimensions of humanness and the ego that is their vehicle, but because they engaged them with a drive and intensity that shook the world to its very foundations. No doubt, they were also plugged into the soul (deeper psychic) and spirit (formless Self) – the ultimate source of their Power – but they expressed that Power, and gave it concrete results, precisely because they dramatically engaged the lower dimensions through which that power could move and speak in terms that could be heard by all.

These great movers and shakers were not small egos; they were, in the best sense of the term, big egos, precisely because the ego (the functional vehicle of the gross realm) can and does exist alongside the soul (the vehicle of the subtle) and the Self (vehicle of the causal). To the extent these great teachers moved the gross realm, they did so with their egos because the ego is the functional vehicle of that realm. They were not, however, identified merely with their egos (that is a narcissist), they simply found their egos plugged into a radiant Cosmic source. The great yogis, saints, and sages accomplished so much precisely because they were not timid little toadies but great big egos, plugged into the dynamic Self, alive to the pure Atman (the pure I-I) that is one with Brahman; they opened their mouths and the world trembled, fell to its knees, and confronted its radiant God!

Beat that if ye can!!

And another thing by me mate Ken

Indeed the whole point is to be fully at home in the body and its desires, the mind and its ideas, and the spirit, and its light. To embrace them fully, evenly, and simultaneously since all are equal gestures of the One and only Taste. To inhibit lust and watch it play; to enter ideas and follow their brilliance; to be swallowed by

Spirit and awaken to a glory that time forgot to name. Body, mind, and spirit, the trilogy, all contained, equally contained, in the ever-present awareness that grounds the entire display.

In the stillness of the night, the Goddess whispers …. In the brightness of the day, dear God roars …. Life pulses, the mind imagines, emotions wave, and thoughts wander. What are all these but the endless movements of One Taste, forever at play with its own gestures, whispering quietly to all who would listen; is this not you your Self? When thunder roars, do you not hear your Self? When lightning cracks, do you not see your Self? When clouds float quietly across the sky, is this not your very own limitless Being, waving back at you?

Bloody hell! I could even hear your voice expressing all of that!

Luv it - Walt

Walter 1999

I am still adjusting to the silence. (Sarah has gone to live with her mother). I've lived alone before so it's not much of a problem, and like I've said before, all the interesting stuff is going on between my ears anyway. However, the fuel for the interesting stuff is coming from somewhere else. It's coming from within, but I can't say exactly what place within it's coming from. If I say it's coming from my heart I would be lying again, and I'm tired of putting out falsehoods. I could say that it's coming from my spirit, but my spirit, if it's not dead already, is at least in the emergency room getting CPR. If it comes back to life it will be drastically changed and will resemble the old one only in as much as it is mine, but this time it will be a much humbler spirit, a spirit more in tune with real life.

Ha! Sounds bad eh? But the funny thing is that it's not bad at all. It's much better than the way it was.

Somehow, somewhere along the way of my tumultuous life course, I turned into a phony. I became an actor. (*All the world is a stage and we are but actors in it.* Shakespeare) My focus in life, now that Sarah is healthy, is on being truthful and in being real.

For me to be entirely truthful to the world at large would only invite more disasters. The world is not ready for truth or tuned into reality, and if I started being truthful and acting real in my social life or at work, I would be ridiculed. So, my focus is on being truthful and real inside myself. (*To thine own self be true and then no man shall find you false.* Shakespeare again)

The truth is I joined the broken-hearted. Do you remember that song; *What Becomes of the Broken-hearted*, well, if they don't shoot themselves or someone else, then they find real life. Then they abandon all acts, all phonies, all the social must-dos and they just sit there. They sit there until reality catches up with them; for reality is much slower than a dream. It's a painful sit, but when reality catches up, we realize that it was worth it.

This writing, and in reading it again, is showing my spiritual journey (to me) and I read what you send me and can see your spiritual journey as well. I'm sure you can see it, Pauline, we are both unravelling from the chain society wrapped us in from birth. As Freddie Mercury sings "I want to break free", this is our spirit singing!

Don't forget that a spiritual journey isn't always going 'up.' Mine certainly isn't. I go up and down and around in circles. Depression is part of our spiritual journey as much as great spiritual insight is. Also, as we write we are identifying the terrible depression that we both eventually went through. In my case, I set it up deluding myself about everything. My worst enemy has been 'fear.' Then my second worst enemy was 'pretence' like pretending to myself that I wasn't afraid, and pretending that I was other than who I was, etc. It has all been a sham!

You did the same! You walked around with a smile on your face. Your kids and others were all fooled by your masquerade. Your fear fuelled your motivations. You didn't want your kids to ever feel the fear you felt as a child under the same circumstances, so you perfected a mask. You were also afraid that your fear would be ripped away and you with others would be made to see who you were which is what happened in the end. Your mental breakdown was necessary as it painfully ripped that mask away, allowing you to be Real! Scary eh!

We are not alone; life is a masquerade for most people. We all hide from ourselves and others. There is a good reason for it too. It is because the way we are doesn't match up with society's model of what a person should be like. The model is impossible to achieve, but do the young souls emerging into this world know that?

I am a human being. I feel everything that a human feels. I go through a full range of emotions from hate to love regularly. I have desires that would be to my benefit, but so do all other human beings, and there are billions of them! All those billions of people, and yet, in all of history, there's only been one who has said, "I did it my way'. It wasn't Napoleon, not Hitler, not Hannibal or Genghis Khan, not even good old Winnie Churchill, it was Frank Sinatra.

Yeah, I'm being facetious, but even Frank died in the end and I would stake my life on a bet that he didn't die in his way.

Do you see what I mean? All those naïve and ignorant masses are being subliminally taught that it's good to do it your way. It must be a noble thing to do because there it is on the radio! And yet they are all being led around like they have a ring on their nose. W.B. Yeats talks about the great hypnotism that envelopes society. It's true too. Every society in every nation is hypnotized. You might say that I live in America, and it's bloody obvious that they are long gone, but the fact is that even the people in New Zealand and Australia are long gone too. They are gone in the opposite direction. And there has never been any further gone, in my whole life experience, than the ones who bought it all, hook line, and sinker, in the North End of Birkenhead right after the war.

We came into being in a country that had a class system, and we came into that class system at the bottom end of it. If that's not a wound to the psyche then what is? In our innocence, we either accepted that the world was right or that it was wrong. If it's right then we accepted that we were inferior human beings, but if we argued with the situation, then we are in for a lifelong inner struggle. Sure enough, an adult can say that the world is right or wrong. But can a child see that? What you are saying is that the world was wrong and that it made its worst blunder of them all when it said that our dad was at the bottom end of anything.

Our five feet two-inch Dad was a giant and as good if not better than the rest of them. We were raised knowing this, but also perhaps because he kept telling his family this.

Anywaze, (as Dad would say) dat's where I'm at.

A couple of doodle poems.
Others doodle but Walter becomes poetic.

Best Time

Mornings are not my best time of day.
Doom and gloom are all I can say.
By lunchtime however my spirits have risen.
I've floated above my sleep-induced prism
and set sail again for that distant shore
of mysteries myths and riddles galore,
Where romance does rule,
and I'm not such a bore.

The Shrink

Ninety per cent of the population is living
In delusion.
Did you know that? she asked.
No, I said.
I thought it was much higher.

Are you deluded? she questioned.
Her eyes bore into mine.
How would I know it if I was?
Just answer me yes or no,
said she.

Yes, I said, I suppose that I am.
Then you are not deluded, she smiled,
Placing a mark on an intimidating clipboard.
Then you surely are! I said with a grin.
Our eyes met again, but I wasn't worried.

I knew she wasn't getting past
The colour
Of my smiling Irish eyes.

But I walked out alone – deluded again

Pauline 2003

In my attempt to explain to others how I felt about Dad, I knew I had to hide how much I feared him as I told the stories of how much I admired him. "You were so lucky to have a dad like that," I would hear so many times from those that read my stories. And I would agree – and still do. But for me, and in looking back, it was like living with a wild animal. We were raised being told his anger was the aftereffect of the war. For all the returned soldier's alcohol loosened the constraint they had placed around their fear of that time they had served in battle. We lived around his limitations and by recognizing them we could then admire him for the rest of his attributes. I can still close my eyes and see his face when he was 'whisky mad'.

I went on to find a man that behaved in a similar way but did physically abuse me and bled me dry financially. I tried to speak to him about his behaviour but never once did he listen or say, I'm sorry, it only fuelled his anger if I tried to speak of what he was doing to us all. Then fear prevented me from living outside his influence, I was afraid he'd find me and kill me if I left and then what would my kids do? I always had to think an action through to its conclusion and would give up trying to talk to him or leave him as my kids would suffer. I can see that the way in which we had been raised formed the way in which I thought about alcohol and anger – I immediately closed down to keep me and my kids safe. Once they were adults, I felt free at last to live my life.

Dad never did harm me physically. I just lived in fear that he would. At those times when he was blind by his anger, I was afraid he wouldn't recognize me as his daughter. So, with Dad, I could love him and fear him. He had been damaged in the war. But with my husband, I ended up only fearing him and love died.

Family Gatherings

Matt's wedding, Walt with Pauline, Johnson, Sarah, Matt & Laura

Walter 2004

In writing this stuff I can see that the North End had a profound effect on me. It's where I start setting up my delusions about myself, like how I begin to cover things up within myself to try to avoid confronting them.

As I see it, these years are necessary for us to fabricate our masks. We go into a period of intense peer pressure and we begin to put on an act that we hope will help us to be one of the crowd. It's often called the rebellious years but it's the conforming years when we start to pretend that we are something we are not to appear 'normal.' The opinion of our peers becomes more important to us than even the opinion of our parents or society at large. It's a time when the games we play as children turn into a pretense that we play for real. To add to the trauma, we also begin to develop our sexual nature, which in turn causes us to put on even more of a false nature so that we fit into a mould that we think will be more successful in attracting the opposite sex. It's a time when our unique individuality is put aside in favour of an image that we think will serve us better. Then comes the workplace where more pressure is put on us to conform and to act like something that we aren't. Naturally enough we relinquish our true selves with the feeling that there is something wrong with it, but we don't admit this to ourselves, we just feel it and try to avoid thinking about it. However, I'm sure that most of us pick up a feeling of inferiority, which in turn we hide from too. We compensate for it by pretending to ourselves that we are superior. Thus comes the inferior/superior complex. Overall, we turn into complete basket cases where we lose all sense of reality.

Anxiety plagues our inner lives along with all kinds of illusions, delusions, and expectations about ourselves and others. I see this period as the first major crisis in our lives. The next one doesn't come until we are middle-aged. The mask we crafted so carefully grows tiresome. It's getting holes in it. Our real self is beginning to pop through it here and there. Sometimes a crisis will blow most of it away and we'll be left staring at ourselves in the mirror where the mask and our true self are giving us some kind of grotesque picture, and that is exactly what happened to me.

My second divorce almost destroyed my mask completely. Yet I still tried desperately to hang on to it. What is staring at me is the realization that I've been a phony for so many years, and what's even worse, I realized that I believed it! That I believed I was the person I pretended to be. And yet I fought to hold onto the mask! I try to repair the holes and rips, but eventually, I can see it's no good, I've glimpsed the truth, and now I can never go back to a life of pretence.

I fell into a deep black hole – depression – an all-time low. My entire world had turned out to be just a figment of my imagination and suddenly, I find myself staring reality in the face. It's not a good feeling! My world had turned into a wasteland. I have no way of managing this reality as it hurls itself at me! I'm like a child again, I'm helpless and hopeless. Yes, I do what children do in that situation and what men and women have done throughout the ages since time began. I cry out! I call for my mother or my father and if no parent is around and we are feeling so very alone in a scary situation we cry out to our maker. Yes, I have done that too and I include you, the one person that saw my masks throughout my life and stayed beside me. You knew who I was beneath my masks but I didn't! How weird is that? The number of times you've tried to help me with words such as – "But you wouldn't be happy if you did that, Walt." And I came back screaming – "Don't tell me what would make me happy or not – you don't know that!" But you did,

Pauline; you studied me as I grew and you had my truth in your hands and I fought you.

Also, I begin to see how I've tossed and turned throughout my life by my feeble and fickle self-will, and I realize I am a slave to my passions, and that I will never be free.

I come to see that none of our passions should ever be destroyed but rather tamed. It is the taming of the passions that help bring out the spiritual being that is inside us, not the destruction of them. We are to become one with all that is, not destroy it. If we admit that we feel the same things that others feel, then it is easier to forgive them. "There but for the grace of God go I!" as Mum so often said to us.

I've concluded that contention is the cause of all our trouble and woes. I find that acceptance of ourselves as we are, acceptance of others as they are, and acceptance that we are not lords of the universe, of other people, or even ourselves, seems to bring me peace. Then most of all I accept the mysterious and unfathomable 'spirit' (God to some) is real and gave me life.

So, like the prodigal son, I begin my way back home. A way that my earthly father pointed to many years ago, not directly, but he pointed to it nevertheless, and in my psyche, he never left me until I was at least started along the way back towards reality. He's just waved me off!

So, after portraying some of the things Dad said to me as being bad, I could see I was fighting him. If he stated that he would give me a million dollars to start a life he pointed me toward, I would have told him to stick it! I was too stubborn and would not take advice because he was my dad and I knew more than him. That hard Irish man had his way of dishing the truth. But it has taken me a lifetime of avoiding the path he tried to push me along and it would have been so much easier to have walked that path and avoided the pain. But would I have learned anything? I try at times to point my kids in a direction that I can see would be beneficial to them, they sort of glaze over their eyes and give me a half smile! Are they any different from me? Like Dad I'm hoping that the pearls of wisdom I've sown from time to time will germinate and suddenly drop into their psyche and they have a light bulb moment, saying, "So that's what Dad meant!" I can only hope.

Recovery
Pauline 2002

In questioning the major breakdown that I'm still recovering from, I see it as a mental breakdown and not a nervous breakdown. My mind knew the signs for the start of my next attack. I'd got to the stage where I was aware that the attack was imminent and 'sucked' my spirit out and up and sat up high watching it happen. I knew my mind and body were in pain but I didn't want to suffer with it! I sat up there telling myself "I'm not going back into that body until the pain is gone."

I was embarrassing you all by talking to your friends when it was obvious I was 'out of my mind'. I even authored a paper about my experience and distributed it to all who knew me. Now I can laugh about that!

From 'up there', I could see and hear all that was going on around my mind and body but was able to choose not to react or take part. That place I lifted my spirit to was painless. I was floating in a sea of beauty. It was also a happy place and I wouldn't have minded staying there permanently. My kids, the doctors, you, and anyone that cared about me were trying to encourage me back 'into my body' – back to sanity, they said – but it was too painful! Why couldn't everyone see that? Once I recovered from that mental breakdown, I wrote a poem trying to explain to you all how I'd been feeling.

You are the only person that understood what I was saying at that time, that being 'out of my mind' was me being sane, I was happier in that space, and aren't we supposed to be happy in this world? And, when I weighed it against how I'd been living where I was supposed to be sane, to me that was insanity – without a doubt, no happiness and extreme pain!

Now that I am supposedly healed – I sneak off and visit my 'out of mind' places, free of the pressure of any kind and I rest and allow myself to be myself! Isn't that how we should be living? Following is that poem.

Sanity by Pauline

Demons start to use me, ripping through my heart and soul,
Fire and knives abuse me – I am dragged across hot coal.
My spirit wraps me in its arms, escaping, starts to soar
and lifts me to another sphere, adrift without an oar.
I see things in my private world that no one else can see, ecstatic
as I'm floating there, my spirit, my world, and me.
I hear what no one else can hear, whispers in my ears, tender
warm and loving words, prompting joyful tears.
Time stands still, life is sweet, Love is all I feel, worldly woes,
stress, and pain, all seem so unreal.
WAKE UP!! Shouting stirs my brain, drags me back to 'life.'
Spirit now releases hold, reality, and strife.
Shocked and maimed, I moan and crawl,
and lose the will to fight,
Fear and pain, stress, and shame, grip my senses tight.
Sanity, must not include, my pleasure-seeking ride,
I'm 'sane' now, no confidence, invisible, I hide.
I look at you, and I can see, *you're* happy I'm 'down here.'
But *I* was really happy while I floated in my sphere.
I'll try to keep myself 'down here' to please the ones I love,
But crazy really suited me, it fitted like a glove.
If I promise not to write it down, or talk to those you know,
Would you mind if I went crazy, perhaps once a month or so?
Because now that I've experienced it, it's obvious to me,
I'm 'normal,' when I'm crazy.
But *I'm* 'mad' in Sanity.

Walter

Freedom

I strove and I struggled to set myself free,
But the greatest of tyrants turned out to be me.
I threw all I could against my desires
But nothing, it seemed, could put out my fires.
Tossing and turning me this way and that.
They ran when I walked and stood when I sat.
I'd laugh then I'd cry, smile then I'd moan
I knew that my life was never my own.
Battered and beaten sickly and tired
From the pit of my heart to the heavens I cried:

IS NOTHING SO GRAND!
CAN NO SUN OUTSHINE
THIS EVIL AND FICKLE
SELF-WILL OF MINE!

A voice very gentle, quiet yet sure
Did whisper an answer: struggle no more.
Submit your desires to my simple plan
And remember for now that you're only a man.
Come let me guide you, be tender and meek
Give me your will and no longer weep.

My eyes were then filled with tears of joy,
I held out my arms and like a small boy
I followed the shepherd, for now, I could see
Surrender is triumph if it's his victory.

Walter 2002

I don't think I've suffered a mental breakdown (or have I? You'd know better than me) but, as far as depression is concerned, I know what you're experiencing. Depression is a terrible thing. Yes, you are right when you say it's the acceptance of the dis-ease that precipitates any kind of relief. If I didn't admit that I'm inclined to depression, then I wouldn't do all the things I now do to ward it off. I feel we both started with depression in our early teen years. Meditation has also been my lifesaver.

Scott Peck said that he needs two hours a day of spiritual exercise and prayer. We are not alone. Many great people and many not-so-great people suffer from this blessed curse. The mind of a depressive is forced to go where others fear to tread! Many famous poets and writers come from our neck of the woods. I'm not saying that I'm a great writer but writing helps me. There is something therapeutic about it. I'm drawn to it like a duck to water. I can't write a letter; I must write a short story! And you are the same! It's why we both must print off our correspondence to each other. So, we can sit back with a cuppa or a beer and read the next story in our lives, sometimes over and over (and then sometimes write back and slam it) but with a guarantee we've given it lots of thought.

Reading has a similar effect on us. Neither of us read for recreation. We read for knowledge, we read to quench a thirst; we read for life. The libraries are full of people like us.

Walter Family 2006

There are things about love that I'll never understand, and there are things about family that I'll never understand. My attitude towards it is *'viva la mystery.'* In a family, we learn to forgive. In a family, we learn to understand each other. There's no exception. We all must go through the usual trials. What brother and sister is there that hasn't fought? A family has the advantage of starting out with love. Not only that, but they also have the advantage of unconditional love. So, it's easier to forgive a member of the family, when they ask for it, than it is to forgive others. It's not only easier but also natural. In a family, we can accept our differences. Members of a family might work in many different fields. They have their successful ones and their dead-beats, but at family reunion times they are all as one. A family is a very valuable thing to have. Like you, I hold the concept of family in the highest regard.

Pauline 2006

I wrote the following piece about family, for my grandchildren.

I ask that you give Shakespeare's quote from 'As You Like It' some thought.

> *All the world's a stage*
> *And all the men and women merely players.*
> *They have their exits and their entrances,*
> *And one man in his time plays many parts,*
> *His acts being seven ages.*

Each of us at any time is a player in another person's drama that they call *life*. We juggle these roles without scripts in their lives, as we play the star in our own drama.

We take part in the many dramas of others for a *reason, a season, or a lifetime*. If it's not a lifetime, then you must learn when to exit gracefully from the stage of another's life drama. You weren't meant to star alongside them through to the end. Don't miss your cue for your entrances and exits.

The people with whom you regularly interact, without any personal commitment, are those that are in your life for a reason as you are for them. Shop assistants, bus drivers, teachers, tradesmen, etc. We help each other meet our needs on a daily basis. Keep this analogy in mind as you interact with those around you but remember that you need to learn from them as they learn from you.

When we have a reciprocal emotional commitment in the parts we play in each other's drama, sometimes this can become overwhelming. But exiting the stage at those points could spoil the drama that is unfolding around us and change its outcome. It might be painful, and we perhaps cannot see the outcome, but we must continue to tread the boards knowing that our bit part is there for a season only. Keep asking yourself *What do I need to learn from this part I play in their life?* You must recognize your cue to exit and let go if/when the time is right.

Those that have ongoing supporting roles in your own drama and you in theirs, and have an emotional connection with you, are there for life, your siblings, your extended family, your children, your parents, and grandparents. They are usually your fan club. They are with you to the end. They are there for a reason and for a lifetime. Learn from them as they learn from you. Plan your drama around them with minimal disruption to their lives and practice sensitive care within your personal drama with them in mind.

A reason – a season – or a lifetime. The drama you star in is your *life* – no scripts, just gut feelings of what the next line should be; you create this drama.

You have graduated from the family university with parents and siblings, you have learned the basics and it's time now to practice all you have learned within the larger family in this world and its people, always remembering that every person of whatever creed and color is part of this family on earth.

How boring would it be if we were all the same, same thoughts, same colour skin, same houses, same cars, and same beliefs? We have this beautiful multicolored family, living all over our enchanting world. With the benefit of our manufactured methods of transportation, we can visit and share in the enchantment of each other's little piece of heaven of which you are a custodian.

Following is my front-page published article in the *New Zealand Herald* newspaper incorporating my family and drama thoughts after the act of terrorism on America's Twin Towers on September 11th, 2001, but acknowledging terrorism around our world.

A Demand to the Elders of this Family
After the Twin Towers Terrorism attack on 11ᵗʰ September 2001

I am a mother in the family of humanity that lives on this earth. I am in pain right now because thousands of my relatives have been senselessly murdered. I live in fear that some of my relatives may use their anger to retaliate which would result in more deaths in my family. I live in terror that my innocent children may die because they are living in the centre of the war zone. We cannot cross our relative's property to escape and they won't take us in to keep us safe.

How did our family ever get into such a state? It is time to stop and witness what we are doing to ourselves.

In the history of our family, we have made many mistakes. War was one of them and it never solved anything.

We have tried "An eye for an eye". It didn't work.

We have "Turned the other cheek". That didn't work either.

To become so angry that we ignore the lessons of our past and repeat them would be ignorant and foolish.

It is time for the elders of our family to stop repeating mistakes and start thinking outside of the square. We must eradicate terrorism but not by losing the lives of any more of our family members. Our elders must get their heads together and find a solution to allow our family to "Live and let live in love and peace in our family home 'The World.'

As I draft this book the elders of this world still have not come to a peaceful resolution to deal with war and terrorism (2023). At this moment in time, we are suffering a war in Ukraine instigated by Russia.

We must always continue reminding and requesting that our elders work to resolve the threat of terrorism and war in our World.

Walter's grandchildren

Josephine and Charlotte, Matthew's children

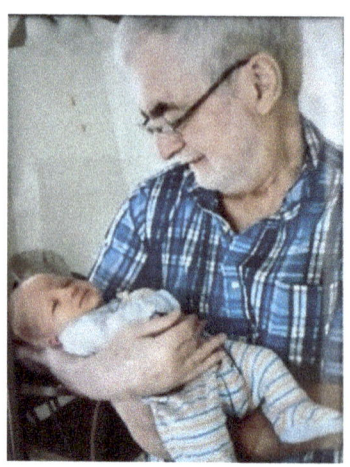

Kiki, Parker & Tyrion – Sarah's children

Walter's grandchildren

Walter's doodle poems

Stranger

I plumb the depths inside me
And pray to the heavens above,
For I've found a dying stranger
Who's only cure is love.

His screams though they are silent
Are felt in my sad heart.
His life is fading slowly
But I vow we'll never part.

Take this mask off from me,
Bare my face to his eyes,
Let me feel his feelings
Let me sigh his sighs.

Together we'll pull through it,
Together we'll fight free.
For I've found a dying stranger
And that stranger's really me.

Oak

The lone oak
Black and bare
Amongst the dancing
Shimmering mist
Has sprouted
A leaf.
And a lark
Is singing
On its bony
Finger
That points
Upwards
To a
Pregnant
Sky.

Walter

I was reminded again that, in a war, soldiers are taught to put their fellow soldiers first, their fighting mates. This has the amazing ability, if it is followed, to diminish fear completely. So, after Dad said that I was scared he also gave me the solution to overcoming fear, and it was a solution that could only come from the military.

I'm being nudged to write again. We've both spoken of this before – writing faces our fears and puts some clarity around them, ready to kick them off the cliff. Writing is as much an exploration of ourselves as it is creative. I have never really known beforehand what I was about to write. It just comes out. I usually always start writing with a blank mind. Just write about the weather, or whatever turns your crank, and within a short while something will happen. I think a connection to the subconscious is made, and then it starts to flow.

I'm wondering if writers have a different nervous system than other people. The part that separates the conscious mind from the subconscious in most people has not occurred in writers. I think we, as writers, still have a clear connection to the subconscious mind. Not only that, but it's like a drawbridge that we can raise up or let down. We raise it up by just writing! It's called the muse. (Definition: *a person or personified force being the source of inspiration for a creative artist.*) Call it what you will, but if it's there and it's calling you, then it's best to answer it or it will drive you mad. I'm not joking. Other people do not and cannot understand it. How could they?

It's a gift. It's something special. We live in two worlds at once.

We are straddled between reality and fantasy. We dream with our eyes open. Our only chance of sanity is to express ourselves, not socially but in an artistic way, and most of all from our gut feelings. Then we will learn who we are and what it is that makes us tick. But we must surrender to it. To whatever that 'it' is. We must allow it to flow right through us.

Why do you think I became so obsessed with freedom and fate? If that is my fate, how can I say I have freedom? I could not see any freedom. I had choices all right, but what were those choices? There was never anything but one choice and I was bound by chains of steel to choose it. Freedom? Destiny? Does sanity choose for me? If I cannot see the choice does that mean I am insane?

The good news is that if I do write, and if I do let it flow through me, then I keep on getting saner. Ha! I must admit, it's better than getting insaner! I suppose one can get used to anything given time. Getting saner means moving toward sanity, and that of course is an acknowledgment to you that at this moment in time, I am insane!

Take care, it's good to know I'm not alone!

Walt x

Pauline

Cheeky Bugger!

Walter doodle poems

I have a friend:
more
valuable
than gold,
more
precious than gems,
more
dear
than
a
lone
drop
of rain
falling
onto
the swollen tongue
of a dying man
in an arid
and desolate
desert.

I have a friend.

Transformation

Blown away by the winds of change.
Illusions bursting like guns on a range.
Realities furnace burning again.
The fear, the sadness, of purity's pain,
And my life fizzing out like sparkling champagne.

Thankful at last that now I can see.
The liar that formed my reality,
And the truth that must work to set my soul free
That truth is in chains,
And it's called mystery.

Pauline

I have been asked often "How can you really love someone you really feared?" But we both did, didn't we? It was too complex to explain all those years back. We really loved this funny intelligent man but shrank into the shadows when he came home after the booze, especially whisky booze. He harmed us emotionally and spiritually but, if he were alive today, he would be mortified if he were told he had harmed his kids in any way. An acquaintance of mine hearing my explanation of my life and feelings for my father said, "You've got to be crazy!" My response was: "Yes, I was" and I now have a doctor's note to prove it!

Walter

Pauline, I love your passion. I love the way you grasp things, and your intellect as well as your honesty in trying to apply it. It's like a glass of water to a dying man in a desert! We can sigh at times asking where did we get this intellect. But I've never had any doubt in my mind that it came from Dad.

He had a way of sowing little time bombs that would explode later in life. Were you there when he told the story that the world out there, up in the sky, might be populated by monkeys for all we know? He often went into conversations with us that were beyond the pale of the ordinary Dad of that time, or any other time, I'm sure. He had our attention all right and we hung onto every word.

I remember when he was working on the high steel when we were still in Carnforth Street. He came home one day and I was messing around with his bike trying to learn how to ride it, and he just walked over to me with his huge grin on his face and gave me half a crown! He said he would give me another half-crown when I had learned to ride it. (He probably did but I can't remember the second one like I did the initial one.) When I got my first black eye, he gave me another half-crown and told me there was plenty more for every black eye after. I was such a sensitive kid, I realized much later in life he was trying to toughen me up ready for the world we lived in. And I'll never forget him bursting out laughing when I finally got some young girl into the hallway of the prefab. It was the classic case of, 'you show me yours and I'll show you mine' stuff. I had already shown the girl mine, and just when she was about to show me hers, I heard uproarious laughter from within the prefab. Dad was cracking up; the girl ran out the door. Then I heard him shouting 'Doris!' I remember being frightened of going into the room and, when I did, he just had that Irish grin on his face with his laughing eyes as he looked at me, but never mentioned it again.

When we chose our seven books we were allowed from the Birkenhead Library (must be returned in fourteen days) and before we would return them, I can remember us all discussing our books with Dad. I sat listening to him in awe, thinking how did he keep all that reading in his head that he'd done over his life? We could ask him anything and he always had the right answer. Or did he? He certainly convinced his kids he knew everything. I felt that, if he didn't have a textbook answer for us, he would verbally talk it through with us until he was happy that we had solved another mystery. There are a lot of things that remind me of his intellect and even his sensitivity. One strange one is: I had found a very rare book in the house on witchcraft, and it said that if one holds one's attention on a certain spot on a person's neck (back of the neck), then one can communicate with that person. So, after reading this, one day, my dad and I were going to a Tranmere game. Dad had left me up for lost, and he was walking up to the bus depot on Laird Street. I was trying to catch him up. I didn't want to yell at him. So, I thought I'd try to concentrate on that part of his neck that I'd just read about. I concentrated hard and, in my mind, said 'Dad.' To my surprise, he stopped in his tracks and turned around. He grinned his usual grin and flicked his head toward the bus stop, meaning, 'Hurry up.' I've tried it many times since in my adult world – it still works.

Pauline

Mum would do that when she saw a black aura around someone in a room. To Mum, this meant the person was evil. She would bore her eyes into the back of their neck until they must have 'felt' it because they would turn around to face her. Then she would scowl until the person couldn't take her judgment anymore and would leave the room. I watched her do this so many times. That book must have been Mum's witchcraft book.

Walter

As for Mum, in my experimenting with drugs stage, when I vividly saw gnomes and other unworldly things right there in our living room, and after I told her this and that I was using drugs, she brought tears to her eyes and stood before me for a couple of seconds without any verbal tirade. Then just held me in her arms and I've never felt better comforted. She drove all those bad gnomes away. She just rocked me like the child I still was in her eyes and gave me strength. It was a strength way beyond any mere words that she could have said. It was much more than words could convey. She *embalmed* me with her strength. She made sure that I had it to protect me, but she never did it in words. And at any time since then, when I've felt emotional or spiritual pain, I can still feel her powerful strength. That *embalming* has lasted my entire life.

When she came to America to meet her grandson that was the first time we had sat together and talked to each other, or the first time I felt she had really talked to me. I asked her why that was. Firstly, she said our home was a busy place with us kids doing various activities, and the door was always open for family friends, and neighbours. She felt she was always there for any of us if we wanted serious conversations, but her kids quickly became know-it-alls and felt they knew more than she did. (I think she was right there!) As we grew, she moved into the role of merely being housekeeper. And that was okay, she said. We all knew she was there if needed in any capacity.

Smee agin'

A snippet of information I've just uncovered. The area we lived in Birkenhead was also a Viking stronghold many years ago. The real descendants of that area come from Celtic or a Viking background. The Celts, of course, were from Wales. Then, when the potato famine came about, the Irish came over in droves. But they were treated like second-class citizens. The same thing happened to the ones that came to America. They were treated worse than animals. Signs were placed in restaurant windows saying, "No dogs or Irish allowed inside." It was common to refer to the Irish as being less than human. The saying 'Beyond the Pale' comes from the English when they took over Dublin, and they had a wall that was called 'the Pale.' Anything outside that wall was barbaric. The Irish were considered, for many centuries, to be the scum of the earth, and the attitude was still evident in many parts of English society when we were kids.

The English do seem to have done a lot of harm to the Irish. However, I do not feel any anger towards the English. I was raised in England and I know full well that they are decent people. My anger is directed at the lies that governments perpetuate and the ignorance of those that believe them. My anger is in no way directed at individual people. I get along fine with almost everyone.

Pauline 2014

Dan Dare (as we called him) if you remember he lost his Mum and Dad at an early age and the council allowed him to stay in his home. You know he married and had two intellectually handicapped children. I have only just heard that his wife left him and the kids when they were babies. He's been raising them himself for more than fifteen years and last week his kids found him dead in bed. They have now been taken into care. Those poor kids! And as for Dan – what a life eh! What was the point of his life? It was such a sad life.

Walter

It's a sad thing to say all right, but the insight I've got into what Dan has been going through over all those years has caused me to change my evaluation of my life. I'm not hard done by! I'm not poor! I'm one of the richest men in the bloody world! I believe many people that knew Dan would be reassessing and comparing their lives against his and feeling the same as me. His purpose was to show people such as me how rich we are.

I mean it's all right churning out platitudes but it's another thing to live what we say! What does it take for us to wake up? You will know what I mean. If we can get it, if we can really appreciate the amount of suffering that is going on, the amount of courage it might be taking for a person to just face another day, then we might face our days with an attitude of compassion for others and then come to realize that our load isn't all that heavy, and we might even go about our day feeling a bit lighter in spirit.

I also know a retired doctor that became overwhelmed by the vastness of all the suffering around him. He couldn't heal it all, so felt he was a failure. He spent a lifetime dealing with pain and death.

I carefully and quietly talked to him. He needed to know that his care for each person he worked with was healing. If it did not heal the physical malady, it was healing that person's soul. Knowing someone cares is a healing balm for the recipient. People such as him are so necessary in our world.

Both of us, you and I, are healers. But the problem is how to heal. What is the best way for us? I go subtle, but others go direct. I have no doubt left in my mind that the reason I write is to show that we all suffer. No one is immune from life's suffering. Suffering is a part of life just as death is. Within the suffering is a lesson to be learned. Learning that lesson places it in your medical bag and can be used in the future to heal another. If one sees this and stays alert and does not sink into self-pity, it makes the suffering so much easier. Our lives are ebbing and flowing; the tide comes in and it goes out. Staying alert through the suffering highlights the times of pleasure between our bouts of 'education'.

Writing is an art, and like any artist, we must become indifferent to the applause to gain anything worthwhile from this craft. But then again, I could be wrong because there is another kind of applause that comes from the inner realm. It comes from every atom that makes up our bodies, and that is the kind of applause the true artist seeks. True art is not a reflection of society. It reflects one member of society, the artist, and if it is done well, every member of society that sees it will feel something when they see it. True art in writing reflects a truth or an emotion that people have been reluctant to admit to. The artist must stand naked and unashamed if he is to warrant the rewards, and the rewards do not come from society. They come from every atom of his body as they revel in the beauty of it all. It is in this way that the true artist finds love, and, in the finding, his natural expression is to show it, and so, the true artist turns into a poet. A poet is nothing more than a person that keeps on showing us the things that we refuse to see that may link us back to the source of happiness.

Suspend judgment. What do we know? Let God judge. All we are asked to do is to be ourselves, the self we were made to be, the self that picks up genes and runs with them. We didn't choose them, but they are there, nevertheless. Like in a game of cards, we must take our hand and play it the best we can. Some people get better hands dealt to them, and some get worse too.

Accept the hand you have been dealt and always strive to do the best you can with it. That is the real challenge of a good life.

Epilogue

After Walter lost his home and all his writings and possessions in the fires of Oregon in 2021, he lived for a short while with his daughter and grandchildren and then rented a unit. From that moment, his strength began to wane. He was hospitalized twice, once with a suspected heart attack and the other with suspected pneumonia. During the second hospital stay, they did many tests as he was shaking badly and it was thought he had Parkinson's, which turned out to be something similar called an Essential Tremor.

He was told it would not improve in any way. This restricted his movements and lifestyle, and his ability to communicate now was impaired. He gave his car and laptop to his granddaughter, Kiki, and she organized to visit weekly with his shopping and doing chores for him.

He was becoming extremely frustrated and depressed as his life closed down around him. As his sister, I knew he was preparing to check out. He died of a heart attack on 23rd January 2023.

The historical emails that I had of his, I have turned into this book. As he said himself: his writings were to show that we all suffer, it's part of living. This book shows how he managed his challenges and are lessons for those that read it. His children were his priority and the reason why he stayed in America.

In one of the last times we interacted, he said, "I've never felt like this world is my home. I've always felt like an ugly duckling here, and I think I want to go to a place where I'm a swan."

When Walter died, spiritually we spent eight weeks together to complete this book. His contribution to the peace movement by becoming a Hippie should be recognised. Though I didn't join a Hippie group, I still lived a life with the same principles of Peace, not war. The lessons he learned from 'life' I have presented to you here on his behalf.

Thank you, Walter, for being my brother and keeping me 'sane' or 'insane' at any one time, but always understanding where I was coming from. I was the lucky one that had you for a brother and you never acknowledged just how special you were as a human being, not just for me, but all those lives you touched throughout your life. You were always humble. The words and ruminations in this book are your contributions to the world. You came here to show us the way. I now believe in your transformation into a swan, and I know you are floating peacefully on your lake, having a well-earned rest, knowing your work here is done. But I will miss you every day for the rest of my life.

I continue my journey with you in my heart and will say,
'Bye for now, Walt, and see you soon."
My Love always!
Pauline

www.ingramcontent.com/pod-product-compliance
Lightning Source LLC
Chambersburg PA
CBHW041140110526
44590CB00027B/4082